MARRIAGE UNCUT

Straight Talk, No Chaser
An Anthology

TENITA C. JOHNSON

 Published by So It Is Written, LLC
Detroit, MI
SoItIsWritten.net

Marriage Uncut: Straight Talk, No Chaser
Copyright © 2018 by Tenita C. Johnson

All rights reserved. No part of this book may be reproduced or transmitted in any form or by any means, electronic or mechanical, including photocopying, recording, or by an information storage and retrieval system - except by a reviewer who may quote brief passages in a review to be printed in a magazine or newspaper - without permission in writing from the publisher.

The Holy Bible, Berean Study Bible, (BSB)
Copyright ©2016, 2018 by Bible Hub
Used by Permission. All Rights Reserved Worldwide.

Scripture quotations marked (MSG) are taken from *THE MESSAGE*, copyright © 1993, 1994, 1995, 1996, 2000, 2001, 2002 by Eugene H. Peterson. Used by permission of NavPress. All rights reserved. Represented by Tyndale House Publishers, Inc.

Scripture quotations marked (NIV) are taken from the Holy Bible, New International Version®, NIV®. Copyright © 1973, 1978, 1984, 2011 by Biblica, Inc.™ Used by permission of Zondervan. All rights reserved worldwide. www.zondervan.com The "NIV" and "New International Version" are trademarks registered in the United States Patent and Trademark Office by Biblica, Inc.™

Scriptures marked KJV are taken from the King James Version (KJV): King James Version, public domain.

Edit by: Shairon Taylor and Darlene Oakley

Formatting: Ya Ya Ya Creative – www.yayayacreative.com

ISBN No. 978-0-9904246-2-8
LCCN: 2018909473

PRINTED AND BOUND IN THE UNITED STATES OF AMERICA

OTHER WORKS
by Tenita C. Johnson

100 Words of Encouragement:
Tidbits of Inspiration

100 Words of Encouragement:
Tidbits of Inspiration – Audio Book

100 Words of Encouragement II:
Driven to Dream

When the Smoke Clears:
A Phoenix Rises

Grammatically Incorrect:
When Commas Save Your Sentences & Your Reputation

From Fatherless To Fearless

The Wait of Success:
How to Become an Overnight Success in 7,300 Days

Available at SoItIsWritten.net and Amazon.com

Table of Contents

Foreword 1
   About the Author: LaShun Franklin, MA & LLP 5

Her Affair, My Fault 7
   About the Author: Jermaine L. Johnson 29

The Ultimatum 31
   About the Author: Tenita C. Johnson 47

False Reality 49
   About the Author: Patricia D. Sims 71

The Perfect Wife for the New Man 73
   About the Author: Robin Burrus 103

Blinded by Love 105
   About the Author: Ortavia McClain 123

Lost & Found 125
   About the Author: Kefentse Booth 143

About: So It Is Written 145

About: The Red Ink Conference 146

FOREWORD
by LaShun Franklin

Marriage. The oldest and first relationship designed in the earth, as we know it. The very foundation of most societies exist because a man and a woman made a choice (or it was chosen for them) to be in a committed relationship. In Western culture, we have many catch phrases that try to describe the journey of marriage. While some are positive, others are negative. However, what it all boils down to is this: *marriage is hard work!*

Many married couples spent more time dreaming about their lives together and planning a wedding than they did preparing for the new job description of husband or wife. Many of us had to figure it out as we went along, evaluating daily if the investment was even worth it! Many of our predecessors hid the work and presented to us a scripted look at marriage, which unfortunately could have never properly prepared us for what came next.

In Matthew 19:11-12, in the Message translation, Jesus has some "real talk" with the Pharisees and His disciples: *But Jesus said, "Not everyone is mature enough to live a married life. It requires a certain aptitude and grace. Marriage isn't for everyone. Some, from birth seemingly, never give marriage a thought. Others never get asked - or accepted. And some decide not to get married for kingdom reasons. But if you're capable of growing into the largeness of marriage, do it."*

Jesus clarifies a couple of things that people need to understand well *before* they enter a marriage. In verse 11, the key is that not everyone is *mature* enough to live a married life. In verse 12, He reiterates his message saying, "Marriage will *grow you up, if you're up to the challenge!"* This is not a negative statement; however, it is a very encouraging one. Jesus is encouraging us to examine our own capacity to love others and please God in doing so. The earlier verses in this 19th chapter support God's original plan for marriage and what standard He is expecting from those of us who choose marriage.

Marriage Uncut: Straight Talk, No Chaser is an "in your face" look at the real work of real marriages. It gives us a very raw and uncut look at the potential situations that every marriage may experience and the decisions that the writers chose when faced with these challenges. Reading this book feels like you are interviewing a couple on a scripted reality television show. Some situations may echo your own, or may mirror the lives of someone you know. You may find yourself laughing, crying or praying with and for these couples as they share their candid truths. The level of transparency may even feel slightly embarrassing, at times, but you will 'get it'! We get to witness the *maturation* and *expansion* opportunities that marriage offers, in the wake of personality differences, mistakes, trials and lack of knowledge.

Unfortunately, we do not currently live in a culture or nation that supports healthy marriage, like it did in earlier years. With a 50-60% divorce rate in the U.S., and the decline of the traditional family, we have to take a hard look at how we can help others make good, healthy decisions concerning marriage. In the many years of providing counsel and mentoring for couples, I have found that good preparation, tools, support and transparency is key to helping couples thrive. In the event that challenges occur during marriage (which they will), having transparent, mature mentors and accountability is golden! This anthology is not for the person who chooses to hide behind the face of religion or fantasy. The uncut nature of their accounts can be used as a teaching tool to provide readers with hope, insight and courage to make better choices in their own marriage.

I leave you with my life's motto: "Marriage is good. Family is good. Marriage is work, and it is a good work. Everything can be fixed, so let us get on with it!"

About the Author
➥ LaShun Franklin, MA & LLP

While many people choose to brush their issues under the rug, LaShun Franklin, MA & LLP, removes the rug altogether, helping clients deal with their issues head on. Realizing that it's often easier for people to hide behind the masks of guilt, shame and error, Franklin works wholeheartedly to usher her clientele into their purpose, passion and prosperity. Specializing in mood disorders, anxiety, ADHD, and grief, she teaches her clients that in order to effectively live, one must die to self on a daily basis.

In addition to holding a Bachelor of Science in Psychology and a Master of Arts in Marriage and Family Therapy, she is also certified as a Limited Licensed Psychologist by the State of Michigan and a Trauma and Loss Specialist. Her tenacity to help clients heal from past wounds, coupled with her educational background, opened doors for her to lead Facilitating Open Couple Communication, Understanding and Study (F.O.C.C.U.S.) and the Prevention and Relationship Enhancement Program (P.R.E.P.). Obtaining ministerial training from Rhema Bible

College, certification from Light University, and her license through Destiny Outreach Ministerial Alliance (DOMA), Franklin has made it her mission to restore broken marriages and families—one client at a time.

Serving as a master-level psychotherapist, she uses a wide variety of theory-based techniques, such as Cognitive Behavioral, Rational Emotive Therapy, Solution-focused Brief Techniques, Play-based Activities and Gestalt Psychology. Through her creative strategy efforts and out-of-the-box problem-solving techniques, Franklin helps her clients realize that success truly happens—not when you have all of the answers to life's questions—but when you are able to face the questions you've been avoiding your whole life.

Understanding that life is often driven by relationships, she coaches couples, families and individuals alike on how to set boundaries, sever ties with unhealthy relationships, rebuild self-esteem and live the abundant life the way God intended. As a master motivator, teacher and purpose coach, she is committed to helping her clients turn their worry and wounds into wisdom. And while many will tell you that time heals all wounds, she will argue that healing—true healing—only comes to those who are willing to peel back the layers and do the work.

For appointments or more information, please email lashun@songsofsolomonri.com or call 313-794-5152.

Her Affair, My Fault
by Jermaine L. Johnson

As I sat twiddling my thumbs in Vision Hall of the church, I awaited Wifey's arrival to confirm something I already knew. I actually got *a vision*. Vision Hall was the main lobby of our church. It was called Vision Hall because the church was the vision of our pastor's father. I'm not sure if the purpose of Vision Hall was for people to get a vision, but I did.

I saw us sharing our testimony with couples who were going through the same thing. Instantly, I rebuked the vision and said to myself, "Nope! Not gone be able to do it! Get thee behind me, Satan!"

As my impatience grew sitting on the bench in Vision Hall, I saw my wife walking up to the door. I got up to hold the door open for her, and she greeted me with just one word.

"Hey."

Though it was only one word, her tone said it all. The low volume of her voice mirrored the low point of her life and the level of embarrassment she felt. The cracking in her voice revealed the pain she was in. I responded to her meek greeting like a lion roaring at his prey.

"Hey, what's up? Why are we here?"

I was ready to pounce on her just to get this awkward situation over with. By this time, our counselor stood over the glass balcony that overlooked Vision Hall.

"Come on up, guys," he said.

It was obvious she had been talking to him the whole time leading up to this day to ensure she wouldn't have to face me alone. As we walked up the stairs, seemingly in slow motion, I felt like a man being led to the chair for execution. I remember thinking, *"God, how did we get here?"* We were pillars in the church. I was a mighty man of God, serving every Sunday and any other day they needed me. Wifey was heavily involved in the youth ministry. She also sang on the praise team and in two of the church choirs. We attended the "In It for Life" marriage Sunday School class when we were not serving. We'd done everything right!

Or had we?

We walked into the same classroom where our marriage Sunday School classes were held weekly. We sat at a rectangular table at the front corner of the room with our counselor, who was also our marriage Sunday School class facilitator. We had history with him. Because he was also a licensed therapist, we counseled with him for months. He and his wife were our spiritual mentors, as well as the head of the family and marriage ministry of the church. One time, they even suggested that we would pick up the mantle from them to oversee the marriage Sunday School class and the family ministry. They were truly like family.

I sat in the far chair with my back against the wall. Who knew this would describe how I would feel minutes later? Wifey sat across from me and the counselor sat to the left of me.

I roared again, "Why are we here? What's going on?"

Wifey, with great intimidation, looked down defeated as our counselor spoke up for her. As he spoke, I honestly can't remember a thing he said, except when he uttered the words, "She went outside the marriage."

Tears instantly streamed down Wifey's face.

I looked at her and asked, "What does that mean? Went outside the marriage? You cheated on me?"

The counselor spoke up again, serving as her voice until she could speak. "Yes. She had an affair."

I bombarded her with questions. Her voice cracked as she tried to answer. Yet, I cut her off with question after question.

"Who was it? How long has this been going on? When did you meet him? Where is he now?"

The answers to these questions didn't matter much. My suspicions were confirmed and, even though I expected it, it didn't make it any easier to digest. Our counselor tried to calm me down as I pounded on the table with two fists simultaneously. With every pound, I could see Wifey jump in fear.

"Why would you tell me like this!" But, deep down, I knew why; she was afraid of what I would do if we were alone. Truthfully, she was right.

She kept saying, "It was a mistake! I messed up!" She was sobbing so frantically that I could barely understand her as she tried to convince me that she was still committed to the marriage. For a split second, I almost felt sorry for her! After all, this is my wife! Flesh of my flesh, bone of my bones. As a true man of God, I knew I should love her as I love myself. But the Word also says that if my right hand causes me to stumble, cut it off. She is right-handed and I was stumbling, so I was fine cutting her off!

"God, how did we get here?"

I continued yelling at Wifey as our counselor morphed back into our Sunday School facilitator and mentor role and said, "Jermaine, remember you're in the house of the Lord."

There was a short pause before I responded to him without looking at her.

"You're right." With a look of disgust and defeat on my face, I mustered up enough energy to make one more outburst. "I'm done!"

Fighting back tears, I got up and walked to my car, feeling like I had just gotten punched in the *family jewels*. I felt like an overweight man who'd run a marathon without any training. I could barely catch my breath and I had chest pains. Was I having a heart attack? Yes, but not the heart beating in my chest. It was the one you draw on a Valentine's Day card.

My heart was broken. How could she do this to me? *To me!* The one who had done anything for her. The one who would still do anything for her! I was the one who quit a good job because she was going through depression after losing our twins at birth the day after our wedding! I was the one working long, crazy hours to pay bills, while she was writing books and couldn't find a steady job! I was the one working and paying her student loans, while she went back to school for a master's degree because she was unfulfilled! I was clearly in the third stage of grief: *anger!*

As I drove home to await part two of this drama called my life, I got a text from Wifey: "We're staying at my girlfriend's tonight. I'll be back to get my stuff tomorrow."

She had texted me earlier before our meeting at the church to let me know she had dropped our only child together off at her girlfriend's to watch during our meeting. That was odd to me because we had meetings before where we simply took him with us. One of us would give him our phone or a toy, and he would be fine to occupy himself during the meeting. Then, it dawned on me. This was premeditated. I was furious!

I got home to our other son, who is my biological son, but Wifey has been his only mother figure. I thought to myself, *"How could she do this to him?"* His biological mother had just passed away a few months earlier and now, he was going to have to lose the only motherly figure in his life to divorce. Then, I thought about our youngest son. He was going to have to grow up in a single-parent home, which I despised. I was raised in a single-parent house, without a father, and so was the Wifey. I had always vowed that I would never put my kids through that. I wanted to be the real-life Huxtables, and she'd ruined that for us.

I arrived home and parked in the garage. I sat there for a moment and the flood gates opened. I cried like a child who had just gotten his first spanking. I was hurt and in disbelief.

"God, how did we get here?"

I got myself together because I couldn't let my son, or anyone else, see me like *this*. I dried my face on an old dirty rag in my garage. With blood shot eyes, I walked in the side door and my son was eagerly waiting for me.

"Did she already tell him? How could she!?!?! That's not her place to tell him!"

As I crept up the steps, I greeted him with the same greeting Wifey had greeted me with an hour before.

"Hey," I said, with the weight of the world seemingly on my shoulders.

"You ready?" he replied, seemingly excited.

Feeling a sense of pride, I felt as if I had someone to help me shoulder this load because he got it! This is my son, who is named after me. So, of course he feels my pain! He was asking me if I was ready for this next stage in our lives! Just me and him against the world, just like the Tupac song!

If only this were true! I'd forgot he had a laser tag party to attend, and I had told him I would take him. I was half right though; it was time for the next stage of my life.

Depression.

I drove my son to the party, in a location we had just been to a few weeks prior. Yet somehow, I got lost. With a look of confusion on his face, my son asked, "Where you going?" That was such a loaded question. Truth is, I really didn't know where I was going. My mind was on everything, but this drive—which should've taken 15 to 20 minutes—took us 45 minutes. All these thoughts rushed through my head. *Who was this dude? Did he look better than me? Was he skinny? I have gained a lot of weight. Was he anatomically bigger than me? Was there oral relations? Did he have an orgasm? Did she have an orgasm? Did she like it? Was he better than me?* That last thought kept resurfacing! It's crazy how you can take an arrogant, cocky, headstrong Marine and break him down with one act. I was one of the few, the proud, the brave— and now, the broken-down Marine!

"God, how did we get here?"

After I dropped my son off at his party, I headed to the store. I was depressed and angry all at the same time! As I walked through the store to find something to help me pack my shi—*stuff*, I found some blue containers. I got as many as I could that would fit into my car. I went back to pick up my son from the party. When he got in the car, he saw the blue containers on the back seat.

"We moving?" he asked me, with a surprised look on his face. By this time, the excitement of the party had worn off and he noticed a change in my demeanor. All this time, I forgot he didn't have a clue about what was going on. I drummed up enough courage to tell him what was going on with me and his soon-to-be ex-mother. I didn't give him the full details, but enough to try and win him over to my side.

We say we don't want the kids to have to choose sides. But, if we're really honest with ourselves, when going through a divorce, we really do want them to choose. And I wanted to look like the good guy. I wanted her to play the villain in this story. But his reaction was just as shocking as the news Wifey had given me. His reaction was … no reaction at all!

We had played this game before with the kids. We'd sat them down and told them that we were getting a divorce, only to work things out and not follow through with it. His response was, "*If* this happens, where will me and my brother be staying at? Here or somewhere else? Are we going to be together?"

I didn't know how to respond to that. I just told him we'd figure it all out later, and he went to play his video game. His only concern was his family being together. Funny how a 14-year-old kid had better fatherly instincts than a 35-year-old man. He had tagged along with me to men's ministry events, and it seemed that he was getting it. But, I didn't. I was no longer asking, "God, how did *we* get here?"

I asked myself, "How did *you* get here?"

My son went to sleep and I was up all alone, with my thoughts. My sixth-grade teacher, Mrs. Cooper, always said, "An idle mind is the devil's workshop." I truly learned the meaning of this that night. I went through fits of anger, rage and depression as I packed my stuff up. Every negative thought raced through my mind. *Every time she went out, and I didn't know where she was, was she cheating then?* I thought back to the most innocent times we had and turned them into a way how she could've been cheating on me. I took breaks from packing to go post something negative on social media about the woman I once had asked God at the age of 18 for. Again, I wanted everyone to be on my side. I wanted everyone to know that she was the Jezebel and I was the saint. She broke up this happy home! I wanted her to hurt, just like I was hurting! I wanted everyone to look down on her, as if that would make me feel better.

This went on well into the morning. I periodically looked back on my social media posts to see how many people had viewed or responded to my rants. I knew it was wrong. I heard that small voice, telling me, "You're gonna regret this!" But, I didn't listen. The old folks used to say, "God looks out for babies and fools!" Well, I wasn't no baby! God had told me before all this started that this would be a testimony. His Word never returns void. So, He sent the one person on earth whom He knew I could have received something from at that time.

Mama V. She is our counselor's wife. She was a mother figure and a person who understood me. God knew that I respected her and would listen to her advice. The mere fact that she was up and on social media at this hour in the morning was simply God's divine order; it had to be.

She inboxed me one thing: "STOP IT!"

She soon called me. Although we only talked shortly, it was enough to let me know that what the Wifey did was wrong, but what I was doing was no better. She reminded me of my role as a husband. It was my job to cover her. She reminded me of what would come to be my favorite Scripture, Ephesians 5:25-27: *"Husbands love your wives as Christ loved the church and gave himself up for her to make her holy, cleansing her by the washing with water through the word, and to present her to himself as a radiant church, without stain or wrinkle or any other blemish, but holy and blameless."* In other words, we as husbands are Christ and our wives are the church. It is our job as husbands to cover our wives with the Word of God, like water. If you submerge a person in water, the water touches everything and will get in every opening.

Husbands are supposed to submerge and cover their wives with the Word of God, just like water. However, you can't cover a person in His living water and not expect to get wet. *…and to present her to himself as a radiant wife, without stain or wrinkle or any other blemish, but holy and blameless.* It is up to the husband to make sure his spouse is a radiant wife, without fault or blame, just as Christ did for the church. The Church turned Christ over to be crucified and cheated on Him with other idols, such as money, reputation, even pride. We cheat on God every time we put making money (our jobs), what people think about us (our social media presence), or even our pride over Him or our marriage.

I took a break from packing to take a stroll down memory lane. The first stop was our courtship. I remember vividly sitting on my bed while stationed in Millington, Tennessee, at the age of 18 as a young Marine. I asked God for her to be my wife. She often mailed me (this was before email and cell phones) the most heartfelt letters. She made a big, bad Marine soft; yet, she had a way of making him feel like a king. She's actually the reason I had all the confidence I had. She was the first true God experience I ever had. I asked God for her, and He actually gave her to me. Even though we had times of separation, we always found our way back to each other, like an old love story in a movie.

It wasn't about her looks, although she was and is *fine*! It wasn't about what she had because she didn't have anything material that I couldn't get for myself. It was truly the fact that I loved who and what she was, and I wanted her for the rest of my life. This had to be God's plan. He gave me the desires of my heart, but I didn't realize what came along with this huge responsibility. I knew that my wife was emotionally broken before I married her because of the multiple molestations she'd experienced. She came from a single-parent home, and she never met her father. She didn't have a true father figure in her life, so how could she know how to treat a husband? I asked God for her and He entrusted me with this fragile heart. God did His part, but had I done mine? Had I loved her as Christ loves the church? I thought of all the times I had yelled at the top of my lungs at Wifey. I thought about how I often let my pride prevent me from apologizing in a heated argument, just to make myself feel powerful over her. I went weeks without talking to her, just to prove a point that she needed me more than I needed her. Instead of protecting and covering her fragile heart, I tried to dominate it into submission. Then, it finally hit me.

That's how I got here.

Two weeks earlier, my son graduated from middle school and we went out to dinner. On the way to dinner, Wifey and I got into some argument, which led to one of our "not speaking" seasons. She had already planned to go to her cousin's graduation in Chicago that weekend. The day before Wifey left for Chicago, I hurt my back. I was in so much pain that I couldn't sleep in the bed because the soft mattress hurt my back. I was in so much pain, but I didn't want to tell Wifey because I didn't want to look weak. Not to mention, we were in our "not speaking" season and I had to win! I broke my silence long enough to give her an ultimatum.

In a calm voice, I told her, "While you're in Chicago, you need to decide if this marriage is what you want. If this ain't what you want, we can sit the kids down and tell them we're getting a divorce. You're not happy and I'm tired of living like this."

As I spoke those words, I could see the emotional pain in her face. Sad to say, that actually made me feel a sense of power over her. Maybe she'd realized how good she had it if she feared me leaving. I had played this card many times before, but not quite like this. Before, I had threatened leaving or just left in a fit of rage. This time, I was a cerebral assassin. I was cool, calm and collective when I threatened to leave. This would show her that I was serious and she would really take it to heart.

The problem is *she did*. Meanwhile, my back was in excruciating pain. I actually thought I had a slipped disc, so I had to go to the ER! Again, we're in the season of "not speaking" and I had already broken the code once to give her the ultimatum. If I told her I needed to go to the ER, it would make me look weak. Nope. I wasn't about to do it.

I'm the big, bad Marine. I'm the man. I can take myself to the ER. I don't need her! I got to the ER and the doctor told me I'd pulled a muscle. It was minor, so a few pain pills and ibuprofen for a few days, and I would be fine. The doctor wanted to give me a shot, which would reduce the pain immediately. But, I couldn't drive if I got the shot. She asked if I could call someone to come get me to prevent me from driving after the shot.

"No," I said, even though I knew Wifey was home and just five minutes away from the ER. The doctor gave me one pill to take once I got home so I could sleep. I got home and took the pill. Wifey was in the bed, faking as if she was sleeping simply because she didn't want to endure any more of my wrath. It happened all the time. When we got into it, we painted the imaginary line down the middle of the bed. She would stay on her side, and I would stay on mine. We both acted like we were sleeping when the other would come into the bedroom to avoid having to communicate. My ingenious thinking also led me to think this back pain could work in my favor to hurt her even more! I knew she had issues sleeping when I wasn't sleeping next to her. Even if we weren't speaking, she had *some* comfort just knowing I was still there.

I decided to sleep on the floor in the living room. So, I took the pill and, as the doctor said, the pain eased enough to allow me to sleep in our bed. Instead of getting in the bed once the pain went away, I decided to move to the couch. If she thought that I was so mad that I didn't want to sleep with her, it would really get to her! So, I slept on the couch, which actually hurt my back even more! Looking back, I realize that I chose to go through the pain just to make my wife suffer. I was cutting off my nose to spite my face.

The next morning, Wifey woke up tired and broken from the lack of sleep and emotional torment I had put her through. As she prepared to leave on a four-hour car trip, alone with no sleep, she broke her silence and said, "I'm getting ready to leave. Love you."

She hoped I would show some type of emotional response. But in my head, I thought, *"I got her to crack, so I don't tell her I love her or to have a safe trip. I don't even tell her I slept on the couch cause of my back."*

The last words I said to her were, "Remember what I said. Think about if this is what you want."

About four hours later, I got a text saying, "I made it. Love you."

I responded simply, "OK."

I believe this is the actual moment she decided to do what she did.

Is this how Christ would treat the church? What if when Christ was in the Garden of Gethsemane, He let Peter cut the soldier's ear off and then kill him so that he could flee to avoid His certain death? What if when Christ was being flogged with the cat o' nine tails, he decided to punish those that put Him there? What if Christ decided to punish the Pharisees, who were the church? Christ didn't punish the church. So how could I rationalize punishing my wife? The very thing I asked God for I had tried to destroy. The very thing that attracted me to her is what I had issues with. Had I been covering my wife in the Word, like water covers something submerged within it? What had I done to purify my wife, to make her holy and blameless? I realized then that *I was the issue.*

I hadn't prayed *with* my wife. I didn't pray *over* my wife to ensure that she was covered. I didn't even pray *for* my wife. Sure, I prayed about her, but I never truly prayed *for* her. How could I blame my wife for something when I didn't do my God-given duty as a husband to make her blameless? Now, I'm not saying she was right or justified in what she did. She is accountable to God, just as I am. But I realized I played a major part in this. When we do wrong, or do something out of God's will, He doesn't punish us. He corrects us with love. God gave us the best example ever about marriage with Christ's relationship to the church.

Christ always showed love, and husbands are to do the same to their wives.

I got married because I wanted to spend the rest of my life with a woman who made me feel like a king. It never occurred to me that I needed to build her into the woman of virtue who God called her to be in Proverbs 31 to make her feel like a queen. I didn't do my part in this marriage. How could I blame her for falling short? It was up to me to make her blameless, and I failed. So I had to shoulder that blame.

It's amazing how God works. As I was all in my feelings, reviewing the epiphany about my role as a husband, Wifey's car pulled into the driveway. I would love to tell you that she came in the house, we talked, hugged and kissed, and lived happily ever after.

But, that's not the case. We did talk and, eventually, we hugged and kissed. But the "happily ever after" was much further down the line. The point of this is to get you to understand the role of the husband in the sanctity of marriage. One time at work, a few of us guys were talking. One guy started talking about his ex-wife with such hatred. Another guy said jokingly, just to get under his skin, "Remember, at one time, you loved her and thought you couldn't live without her." It was funny but true at the same time. When most of us get married, when we enter into the three-fold covenant with God and our spouse, we truly feel loved. We don't want to live without our spouse. I know that, if we do our jobs as husbands, our wives *will not cheat*.

The sanctity of marriage is perfect. The only thing in marriage that is not perfect are the two humans who enter into it. However, if we do everything according to the Word, we will have a perfect result. Now, that is still a hard task. We will fall short in one area or another. But before you start looking at her faults, do what God has called *you* to do as a husband. Every mistake that has ever happened on this earth can be traced back to a man not fulfilling his duties as a husband, starting with Adam not covering his wife, Eve, with the Word. The good thing about it is that we have God's grace to recover.

Today, my wife and I serve in marriage ministry and work diligently to restore broken marriages and families. It wasn't an easy road, but we made a decision to stay together and deal with our issues head on. There is no offense that we cannot recover from or forgive. Christ endured literal hell for the church (His bride). He was spit on, cheated on, betrayed, lied about and, ultimately, put to death for the church (His bride). He gave his life and still came back for the church with forgiveness. There is nothing our bride (spouse) can do with remorse that cannot be forgiven.

Our marriage is far from perfect, but it's better than it was when we said, "I do!" So, to every husband I can say wholeheartedly that whatever you're going through in your marriage, know that you can get through it. God would not allow it to happen to you, unless He knew you could handle it. It may not be easy. It may bring you to tears sometimes. But the greater the test, the greater the testimony.

And this is my testimony.

Straight Talk, No Chaser
SELF-REFLECTION

1. What was the most hurtful offense your spouse did to you that you can never forget?

   _____

   _____

2. What part did you play in it?

   _____

   _____

3. How could you have handled it differently, no matter how small, to prevent the offense?

   _____

   _____

4. What was the most offensive thing you have done in your life? It could be something only you and God know about.

   _____

   _____

5. Was the most offensive thing you've done unforgiveable to God?

   _____

   _____

About the Author
➥ Jermaine L. Johnson

While many men marry for reasons that are self-serving, he knows that the true art of marriage is found in serving your spouse. For Jermaine Johnson, author and mentor to many, the verse, "Husbands love your wives as Christ loves the church" isn't to be taken lightly. It's his mandate. His mantra. It's what he stands on when times get rough and what he teaches to men young and old when he's presented with a problem. As a visionary and true man of God, he seeks to heal broken marriages and families to restore God's original intent of marriage back to the Kingdom of God.

The Ultimatum
by Tenita C. Johnson

"**Well, I'm about to go,**" I said as I dragged my bags to the side door, which he didn't bother to help me with.

"Hey…" he mustered up to say from the couch, where he'd slept for the past four days.

Like he did many times before I got on the road, I thought he wanted to pray. Maybe he wanted to talk about "it" before I left. He wasn't going to let this fester over the weekend while I was gone. What he said next both surprised me and sent a shock to my heart. I'd heard it many times before, but this time, it was *different*. Almost prophetic.

"While you're in Chicago, you need to decide if this marriage is something you want," he said coldly.

In times past, he asked me, "Is this marriage something you want? Are you happy?"

My quick response was always a solid, "Yes, I do!"

But, this time, in the darkness of a living room with only the light from the television shining on his face, I simply hung my head. At this point, I wasn't sure what I wanted. I knew I didn't want marriage like *this*. It was common for us to go days, even weeks, without speaking. We could sleep in the bed with an imaginary line of demarcation, which both of us knew not to cross. We could communicate just enough to know who was picking the baby up from the daycare and cooking dinner for the kids, yet still be so very distant from each other.

As I drove four hours to Chicago from Detroit, I spent the majority of the time on the phone with a friend. Venting. Praying. Venting even more. And she asked me the question he'd asked me many times before. That one I seemed to have an immediate answer for before *this time*.

"Do you want your marriage?"

"Honestly, I don't know. No, not like this. If this is marriage, I'm good. I can't live like this."

As I approached the Chicago Loop, I got off the phone with her to meditate, to pray, to think. In addition to me just needing to get the hell away from the stress of home life, I was also back in my hometown for my cousin's high school graduation. His mother, who was my aunt, had passed when he was only fourteen years old. So, it was vital that as much of the family who could be there be there to support his big day. The graduation wasn't until Sunday afternoon, but I drove over early Saturday morning.

When I arrived at my cousin's home, as always, I was welcomed with open arms and love. To them, I'm just Tenita (though they call me Ta-ni-sha). I'm not the bestselling author. I'm not a motivational speaker. I'm not a mentor or marriage ministry advocate. I can go home and just be *me*. If I want to be silly, I can be silly. If I want to say something off the wall, I can say it without judgment or side-eye comments. They know I've written books, and many of them have purchased my books to support. But to my family, I'm just me. I don't have to wear masks or put on facades. I can be the authentic short, loud-mouthed girl from the westside of Chicago.

Even though Chicago is up the street and around the corner from Detroit, I'm not "home" as often as I'd like. So when I do drop into town, it's always a time of celebration. My family cooks a huge meal and, of course, we hit up the hometown favorite pizzerias and Mexican restaurants. We invite family and friends over to one person's house and it's sure to be a big party. I had every intention on having a great time away from the stress, away from the fight, away from the constant battle of marriage. I was in the ring, but I was tired of fighting. Honestly, I wasn't even sure what title or reward I was fighting for anymore.

When one of my younger cousins, Mark, came to see me, he brought his best friend, Kyle. I'd known Kyle most of my life because he and my cousin grew up together. They ran the streets together and did their dirt together. When you saw Mark, you saw Kyle. They'd even traveled to Detroit together a few times to visit Mark's dad, who was deceased by this point unfortunately.

It was no secret to the family that Kyle had a crush on me.

So, whenever I came around, he'd ask, "Are you still married?"

"Yes, Kyle. I'm still married."

"But the question is: Are you *happily* married?"

Pause. The enemy is so strategic with his schemes and tactics. This has to be the oldest pickup line in the history of mankind. This question subliminally implies that if a woman says, "No," or she can't answer at all, that the other man should move in for the opportunity. I didn't want to send that signal, but I didn't answer the question either. I simply laughed it off and continued playing cards as I sipped my Moscato. Throughout the day, Kyle made it clear that he'd been following my life's journey even though he wasn't in it.

"I heard you lost twins. I'm sorry to hear that."

"I saw you wrote another book! Congratulations!"

"You write poetry, too, right? Spit something for me right quick!"

Unpause. At this point, all communication with my husband had ceased for the past week, at least. Here I was, in another state, with a man who could run down my life story for the past ten years; yet, my husband didn't seem interested in any of that. All that rang in my head over and over again was his command, his cold statement, his ultimatum:

"While you're in Chicago, you need to decide if this marriage is something you want."

My head told me that I still wanted the marriage, but my heart wasn't quite sold on the idea.

As the night progressed, my female cousins got dressed up to go to a club. I wasn't in town for that. I'd had my fair share of clubs in college, so I wasn't interested in dressing up to go party only to leave smelling like smoke. They tried numerous times to get me to tag along, but I insisted on staying in for the night.

Red flag number one.

Eventually, I took a ride with Kyle to the city to pick up a "package" of some sort. On our way back to my cousin's home, we were pulled over by Chicago PD. I wasn't driving, so I'd inadvertently left my purse with my ID at my cousin's home. This was when I learned not only was Kyle driving around on a suspended license, but also that he had a gun inside the vehicle. Of course, when the police finally approached the vehicle, the officers asked us both to step out of the vehicle.

"Do you know he's driving on a suspended license?" one of the officers asked me.

"Officer, I'm here from out of town. He's a friend of my cousin's. He was just dropping me back off at the house."

"Well, he can't drive away. I know you don't have your license on you, but you're gonna have to drive away. We can't let him drive away on a suspended license."

I wasn't sure if he was going to jail and I didn't know how to get back to my cousin's place. When the officers released us, I knew there was a God in Heaven. Yet, once again, I chose to ignore His warning.

Red flag number two.

When we made it back to the house, no one was home but us. We sat in the living room, talking and drinking.

"You inspired me! Maybe I'll write a book one day." Okay, he was laying it on too thick now.

"You're beautiful! I know you're going to do great things. You're going to go on to be somebody famous."

Pause. The enemy knows just what to say and when. The enemy already had a foothold in my marriage because we'd made an intentional decision to shut down communication for over a week. So, the enemy made an intentional decision to take advantage of the situation and bridge a wider gap between us. I knew that my love language is words of affirmation, but I was blind to see what the enemy was setting me up for. My husband hadn't talked to me for days, let alone told me how beautiful or pretty I was. He supported my book projects, but it was almost as if he saw it as a hobby, not a career. It had been a while since my husband has spoken greatness over me or encouraged me to pursue my dreams. And it had been ten years since the loss of the twins, so we didn't even talk about it. But here was an outsider, a family friend, who lived miles away, who managed to keep tabs on my life's tragedies and triumphs. I was more than impressed. I was drawn to him.

My heart was turned toward him.

Unpause. Suddenly, there was a loud knock on the door at 11:45 p.m. It was my cousin Johnathan who was graduating the next day. It was clear he'd been drinking and could barely stand up. He came in the house, staggering, murmuring words neither of us could understand. He asked me several times to take him home, but I refused. It was late. I was tired. He was drunk and just needed to rest up for graduation the following day.

But perhaps, that was my third, and final, warning.

Red flag number three.

What came after a 12-hour day of full communication with another man outside of my marriage was, at that point, a *choice*. It was a mistake, but it was a choice. I had made an "oops," but it was a choice. Walking upstairs into a dark hallway and even darker bedroom, I came to the conclusion that I no longer had anything to lose.

I'd already lost it.

My marriage was over.

I felt undervalued, unappreciated to say the least. My husband and I had considered divorce too many times to count. But *this time* was different. Something died on the inside of me as I walked out of the house that morning on the heels of his untimely ultimatum. It was clear I was fighting a losing battle, and I don't like losing. I knew how to fight, but I didn't know how to fight fair. Neither did he. Love wasn't enough. Prayer wasn't enough. Maybe this wasn't the man I was supposed to marry. Maybe I'd missed God. Marriage couldn't possibly be this hard.

So, I chose to get out of the wrestling ring. And in the midst of what happened that early Sunday morning, my marriage, my children and my family's faces flashed right before my eyes.

"God, what did I do?"

The Morning After

I woke up, hoping, praying that what took place the night before was just a dream. But it wasn't. I'd indeed taken it upon myself to step out of the marriage—the one I already had one foot out of anyway. I attended my cousin's graduation and celebrated with the family on Sunday, but I still felt off. I'd lost a piece of me. Something was off kilter. Knowing the guilt, the shame, the error of what I'd done, I instantly wished I could un-do it! I texted my husband.

"I love you."

No response.

That wasn't uncommon. We weren't speaking before I'd left Detroit, so why would he respond to a text message?

By Monday, on my drive back to Detroit, I had to make some phone calls. I wanted to repent. I needed to repent. But I wasn't even sure what that process entailed. I called my college friend, Mya, who told me something I wasn't ready to hear.

"If you don't tell him, the enemy has a foothold over you. You have to tell him, Tee.

This is definitely not something you want to hold in. When he finds out years down the line from someone else, it will be ten times worse."

My heart hit the floor of my vehicle as I let up on the gas pedal to drive slower to my dreaded destination. She had to be crazy. *Tell him? Tell him!* Clearly, she was saved, but she couldn't have been hearing from God clearly. She was trying to get me killed!

But the next week proved to be in her favor of opinion. I was vomiting and sick to my stomach daily. I couldn't look my husband in the eyes. I really couldn't kiss him, hug him or be intimate with him. Every time I took a shower, I tried to scrub "it" off. The scent of another man. The residue. The shame. The guilt. Nothing took my sickness, my uneasiness away. By Wednesday of that week, I called our marriage counselor to ask if he would serve as mediator when I told my husband that I had indeed stepped out of the marriage.

Our appointment, which was that Friday evening, was almost a week to the day that I'd committed the unthinkable sin. At this point, I just needed to sleep. I wanted to eat without vomiting. I was willing to accept the consequences and serve my time—even to the point of divorce if that's what it came to.

It came to just that. *Divorce.*

We'd stood at divorce's door numerous times, threatening to call lawyers and split savings accounts in half so we could both move on and live happily ever after *with someone else*. But, even though we made 529 (or more) threats of divorcing, we'd never come this close. This time, I knew it was over. I knew I'd made the biggest mistake any wife can make to a man who loves his family and children.

As I told him in a classroom of the church we got married in that I'd had an affair, his reaction was exactly what I thought it would be. Anger. Rage. Hurt. Disgust. The look he gave me made me feel like a strange woman who'd just abused his children. He looked like he wanted to hit me, but he didn't. He abused the table with his fist instead.

"It's over. I'm done. I don't wanna hear nothing else."

And just like that, he stormed out of the classroom, down the stairs to the church parking lot, where I soon heard him peel out of the holy place on two wheels down the street. I didn't know where his head was, so I stayed with a friend that night.

Saturday morning when I returned to the house, he'd packed up half of the house—and hadn't slept for more than 24 hours. When I walked into the house, he asked me one question.

"Why? Why would you do this?"

In my hurt, fear and sadness, I couldn't muster up an educated answer to validate the sin, nor did I think it would make a difference at that point.

"I'm sorry! It's just not fun anymore!"

To the average person, that may sound elementary. It may sound immature. But the reality is once you've lost your laughter, once you've lost your inside jokes that only you two share and understand, once you look at each other with sorrow instead of butterflies—you are heading toward a spiritual and natural death in your marriage. It wasn't enough for me to go to work and come home, cook for him and the kids, clean, then go to bed and do it all the next day. We weren't living. We were merely *existing* in the marriage.

By Saturday night, his rage had shifted to reminiscing about the good times we did have. He wished me well on my journey and we agreed that we would tell our friends and family that we simply could not settle our differences, so we decided to divorce.

Even in the midst of the hurt and pain I'd caused him, *he covered me*. He was my covering even in my sin, much like Christ is for the church. Saturday night, he slept in the basement (after several drinks to numb the pain) and I slept in the bedroom. He packed up the house but couldn't move right away.

By Sunday morning, something *shifted*. Something *different* happened. It was Fathers' Day. Early in the morning before church, I heard him knock on the bedroom door. He stood on the wall and asked me several questions that he thought would make him feel better—but actually made the situation worse. He wanted details. Play by play. I felt like I owed it to him.

I felt like that was the least I could do. But, little did I know, little did he know, that did nothing but pour salt on an open wound.

After his interrogative interview, the next thing he asked me stunned me. I was shocked. Numb. Dumbfounded. Confused.

"Can we pray?" he asked. "God told me to come upstairs and pray over my wife."

Here I sat, thinking that I was free. Off the hook, so to speak. I was out of the continuous cycle of "fighting the good fight of faith" in marriage. We'd divorce. He could see the children whenever he wanted. But I had done the ultimate—in response to his ultimatum. But the ultimatum was the final tipping point; it wasn't the root cause. We had years of ineffective communication, financial problems, blended family woes and weeks of not speaking to each other to build this bridge between us. The ultimatum was just the final breaking point for the net.

Yet, here he was—not only ready and willing to forgive—but still willing to cover me as his wife and love me as Christ loves the church. There's nothing Christ won't do or give for the church. He gave His only son as a sacrifice to restore relationship between the Father and the church. There is nothing that can separate us from the love of Christ, no matter how bad the situation appears to man. We prayed and spent the day as a family celebrating him as the wonderful father that he is. *Could God restore my marriage after infidelity?*

The next six months were rocky. Some days, he loved me and wanted to give me the world. Other days, he reflected on the past events and became enraged—to the point that he'd suggest separation or divorce yet again. He was indecisive, to say the least. But eventually, he decided the pain of losing his family, the pain of seeing me with someone else, the pain of another man possibly raising his children in another home would be greater than him staying and working through it.

Today, we facilitate marriage small groups in our home and we serve in ministry under a Marriage Bootcamp, a ten-week course where couples come to transform their marriages under the teaching of godly principles. Our marriage is far from perfect. We've still got a lot of work to do—as a couple and as individuals. But now, we don't sweat the small stuff. We pick up socks. Whomever gets home first cooks dinner. When money is running low, we don't point the finger. Instead, we pray for financial wisdom and that God would make provision. We pray together every morning before my husband leaves for work and before the children head out the door for school. We set the tone of our home by playing worship music daily and lighting scented candles. We hope and pray that everyone who enters our home leaves better than they were when they came in the door.

Now, when couples call us with marital concerns, we can encourage them from a place of wisdom and authenticity because of all we've been through. More than anything, we are living proof that if you want your marriage to work, *if you make a choice to make it work*, it can work. It can be transformed. It can be brand new. We don't have a restored marriage. We have a *renewed* marriage. I have a new love and appreciation for my husband because he did stay and cover me as Christ covers me spiritually. Early on in the marriage, I often wondered if I'd married the right one. Maybe I missed God.

But now I know, without a shadow of a doubt, that this man was handpicked by God for me. And he is fully committed to loving me unconditionally—just as Christ loves the church.

 ## Straight Talk, No Chaser
SELF-REFLECTION

1. What does forgiveness look like for you in marriage?

   _____

   _____

2. What's your limit on what you will and won't forgive in marriage?

   _____

   _____

3. Which one of the spouses caused the affair in this story? Explain.

   _____

   _____

4. How do you rebuild a marriage after an extramarital affair?

   _____

   _____

5. If you encountered a couple who was experiencing this level of turmoil in their marriage, what outside resources would you suggest to them?

   _____

   _____

About the Author
➥ Tenita C. Johnson

From losing a set of twins the day after she and her husband were married, to years of unemployment, suicidal thoughts and blended family woes, she soon learned that the only way out of every fire is to go through it. After going through the fire numerous times, and coming out unscathed, she realized that every fire was orchestrated by God to burn some things off of her to make her better. Not only that, every fire gave her a greater testimony to share with others who may be encountering the same things.

Through her books, Tenita encourages readers nationwide to know that with every test comes a predetermined victory. The young girl who once thought she wasn't good enough has blossomed into a woman of faith who knows that, with God, she is more than just enough. She makes a deliberate choice to live her best life now and walk in her God-given purpose daily, and encourages others to do the same.

For more information or booking, visit www.soitiswritten.net.

False Reality
by Patricia D. Sims

I met my husband in high school, but we were far from what I would consider to be high school sweethearts. In between classes, he followed me around the halls, talking to me and even offering to carry my books. I often declined, thinking, *"Who does that in the 80's?"* He was such a sweet boy, but he'd turn into a firecracker when it came time to defend the people he loved.

He often talked about being bullied as a young child and people often questioned his sexuality.

I thought because he was so bowlegged that when he walked fast, it appeared that he was switching. I never questioned his sexuality, though. Girls were crazy about him and he was definitely a lady's man. As time went on, we dated other people. Yet, we remained close friends. I'd call him to go to the mall or to grab something to eat. I'd even call him to watch a movie.

He was instrumental in me securing my first job as a teenager because the managers liked him and his work ethic.

As years passed, I dropped out of high school and had my first child a few months later. My future hubby brought me clothes that were too big and hand-me-downs from his siblings.

It was the thought that counted and I didn't want to hurt his feelings. When my graduating class of peers was walking across the stage, I was securing my GED. We hung out again. But this time, it was different.

This time, it felt right to date him. During the courtship process, part of my responsibility was driving on date nights. I also had to drive to any other appointments because his car was usually not working, which was unfortunate for a person with mechanical skills. He was a father now, too, so the majority of his money was going toward caring for his son. He continued to be a faithful church member and musician. Anyone can see or hear that his hands were blessed. More importantly, he was excellent with my daughter. He appeared to be a good father to his son as well. I saw his son any time I picked him up from his family home on our way to hang out.

As his good friend, I heard stories about how unhappy he was. He shared that he was just at the house to keep his son while his son's mother worked. He was waiting on an opportunity to leave permanently, but he didn't have a ride to move his personal belongings. Guess who picked him up from the home that he and his ex cohabited? With that nightmare now over, as he referred to it, approximately six months later, we were married.

I will admit. I had an agenda. I wanted a son. But, more importantly, I wanted to be married this time around. My firstborn was born out of wedlock, which was frowned upon. My own family members judged me terribly because of it. So I had this overarching pressure to have children *the right way* next time. Ideally, it would have been nice to have love as the binding factor when we married, but love was not there initially. However, I was convinced that love would surely come. The only marriage experience I had was the observation of marriages around me, which were few and far in between—and mostly *unhealthy*. The very people who were pushing, preaching and teaching us that it was, "better to marry than to burn" (1 Corinthians 7:9) never offered to teach us *how* to be married, let alone how to *stay* married.

Soon, we looked into purchasing a foreclosed home on a land contract. Neither one of us had trust funds or a key financial education. Both of our credit scores needed work, to say the least. However, when the previous tenants vandalized the home, this plan fell through.

So, we decided that he would move into my family's home with us. There was just one thing: the only way a person of the opposite sex could live in the family home was if they were married and showed proof of the marriage. This family clause alone expedited the day we said, "I do!"

The day before our planned trip to the Justice of the Peace, I received a phone call during my shift at the bank. My fiancé was sobbing on the other end.

"I need to tell you something. Promise me you won't leave me."

This kind of behavior almost never yielded good news. It didn't sound like anyone had died, so I heard him out. After some back and forth, he disclosed a fact that I wasn't exactly prepared for.

"I have four children."

Shocked, confused, in tears and out of words, I calmly ended the call. I returned to my post at the drive-thru lane window, shaken. But I couldn't let my coworkers know that I was devastated. *Four kids? How? How did he have all of these children and I only saw one of them consistently?* More detailed conversations ensued that evening, with him promising me that life would go on as we'd planned.

"The other children will be moving out of state soon and all will be well!"

We made our vows at the Justice of the Peace, as scheduled. What I wasn't ready for was the tumultuous roller coaster ride, which was subtle, but began almost immediately. The verbal and physical altercations were not far behind the day of our wedded bliss. The first physical encounter left me lying on the kitchen floor, with blood pouring onto the multi-colored floor tile. I was in my first trimester of pregnancy with our first child together. This incident yielded me twelve stiches to the forehead. He left me there to fend for myself, with my minor daughter.

He returned to the refuge of his family home. I battled with whether I should stay or go. Hours later, he returned to the home, full of remorse.

I forgave him.

This incident shook me to my core. It weakened me. Self-doubt took refuge within me. This man who had never as much as raised his voice at me before had affected me in a manner in which no man had ever done before. Perhaps the absence of my biological father, whom I'd seen only once, executed the initial slap in my face, figuratively. I was better than this; but I didn't have enough confidence to walk away, without feeling like a failure. I sought the advice of older male relatives, who advised me that these types of things occur in a marriage all the time. Perhaps it was me witnessing my grandfather hit my grandmother on more than one occasion. Maybe it was because of my aunts calling the house complaining to my grandmother about the abuse they experienced. Maybe it was the memory of my uncles with stab wounds from their spouses that made me accept that this may be part of marriage.

Luckily for me, this type of incident never occurred again. Violence came in other forms, such as verbal abuse, verbal threats, broken property, a busted dashboard that he beat with his fist and sudden stops on the brakes.

A few years into our marriage, I was summoned to a meeting with the hubby and his ex. His ex was the mother of all four of his children. To my knowledge, prior to this meeting, the visits between the hubby and his children were far and few in between. He blamed her for not allowing him to see their children. The visits that did occur allegedly only took place at my husband's mother's home. It was rumored that the children would be dropped off with nothing but the clothes on their backs for days. The children's grandmother would call my hubby, letting him know that she could not afford to feed the children, along with her multiple children still at home. Many people felt like I was to blame for my husband's lack of involvement in his children's lives, which was completely false.

On a good day, his mom rarely spoke to me. She always told me that I thought I was better than her because I did not allow my children to stay at her dilapidated home, which I was not welcomed into. Once I learned of these exchanges of the children, we kept them on the weekends at our home. About a month into our visits, we had a meeting and were asked to keep the children full-time until their mom's next house was ready. They moved quite often, leaving friends, clothes and toys behind most times.

During the meeting, everyone was flat, nearly blunt. It was as if we were planning a funeral. Hubby left it all up to me to make the final decision. According to rumors, I was the reason he did not have a relationship with them in the first place. So, I knew I had to choose wisely. If it were all left up to him, I would hope that he would not hesitate to give the children a home. Naturally, I agreed. What's two weeks of driving across town, in the snow, to cart the kiddos to their school district until their new home was ready?

Two weeks came and went. I never guessed it. I never saw it coming. Two weeks turned into a trying six years. Instantly, we were a blended family. I spent years wondering, *"What mother abandons her children?"* As the saga unfolded, I questioned if she abandoned them at all. Did the two of them plan this? Did she give him an ultimatum? Did he say that he could take care of the children? After all, we were faring well financially at the time. According to the hubby, their mom was nowhere to be found. She had moved away from the last known address. Her phone was disconnected and we suspected that she left the state to reside with family. The children came into the home with less than polite manners.

"Dang! She's got a big booty!" one of them said. The children constantly looked disheveled and wet the bed. They tended to steal and store food. The children had cognitive delays and were failing academically. This was the total opposite of what I was accustomed to. *What had I got myself into?*

Infidelity played its part in the dissolution of my marriage ultimately. There were receipts for the new purchase of pagers, unexplained whereabouts and sexually transmitted diseases. A woman's intuition is usually on point, but only if she is receptive to what she sees. When I confronted the hubby, naturally, he denied all accusations and offered excuses. He even claimed to be spending the night at his mother's home on several occasions. I tolerated a lot, trying to make this marriage work. But, after a while, with no relief in view, I came to the conclusion that I am no fool. Two can always play that game.

An old boyfriend was "sniffing at my dress" anyway. I was in middle school when we met. He was five years my senior. This man has always made me feel like I was the only girl in the room. He was gainfully employed and well-groomed. He told me years prior that he would always be there for me. By this time, there were two additional children, young infants in the home who were a year apart. We decided to allow the hubby to work full-time while I stayed at home with the seven children. I could work part-time through a temp service to help, as needed. I was emotionally entangled with this guy. He was an escape from this unsuspected nightmare I was living. He listened to me. He validated my gripes. Occasionally, he wrote me letters. He left single flowers on my windshield and constantly offered to make me dinner. He said all the things a girl needs to hear when she didn't have her father or a male role model in her life.

I eventually took the bait. One day I gathered up the courage to take my special friend up on his dinner offer. That night, I was supposed to work. But, I told my only good girlfriend of my plans to meet up with him. I honestly thought that the hubby would never suspect what I was doing, but he did. I later learned that he pressed redial on the phone and my "good girlfriend" informed him of everything. Naturally, that dinner evolved into a full-fledged physical affair that night. I was awakened to the sound of my husband's voice screaming my name.

"Come out! I know you are in there!"

Shortly after, my friend called out to me a couple of times before retrieving his gun. I gathered my thoughts and my wraps, and I proceeded to follow my friend down what seemed like a mile-long hallway, which led to his front door.

He proceeded to pull the door open as he stood behind the door with the gun. I stood face to face with my angry husband. I was still trying to figure out how he knew I was there at all. I intentionally parked my car behind the huge house, out of sight of the residential street. Luckily for me, the police arrived before we spoke a word to one another.

One of the policemen facilitated the verbal exchange. By the time they heard some of the events that occurred, rather bewildered and irritated by the facts, the police ordered us to leave the home. I did the walk of shame out of the door, down to the car and drove home. I never claimed that I was without fault. I thought I would have felt vindicated after the emotional oppression.

Yet, I was still empty. Void. My friend called later that day to assess the outcome after the incident. In that moment, I realized that he was not the answer. I was also quite upset with him for not standing up to my husband and whisking me away to happily ever after. Years passed before my ex and I would briefly cross paths again. We greeted each other with small talk and never communicated again.

The reunion at the house just minutes after being dismissed by the policemen was a teary-eyed one. By this time, the sun had risen. I arrived home last to find the hubby outside, smoking a cigarette—something he swore he did not do. He was putting his things in the car. We absolutely should have parted ways that day. We had so many strikes against us.

But we *stayed*. My ego did not want to be the blame for ending our marriage. I felt that the hubby would get a get-out-of-jail-free card after committing his crimes of infidelity. It was my turn to come back remorseful. And I did.

Lies, stealing, cheating, drinking and more babies became the foundation of our marriage. Alcohol ultimately became my motivation to wake up to face the day. It was also what numbed me so that I could sleep through the night. Hubby knew of my alcohol regimen and enabled my routine by making sure my supply did not run out. I soon went back to work since his income was being garnished for child support. After multiple trips to the Family Independence Agency and Friend of the Court, we learned that the children's mom had been receiving benefits for the children while they were living with us. Even so, his arrearages were so far behind for four children that his $1,800 to $2,000 per week net was reduced to $97 on a good week.

As usual, we turned to our faith. Nothing else was going right. We made the church that I was attending as a young adult our church home before we married. Pastor and first lady were honorable and upstanding people. Hubby was able to supplement his income as a musician, which ultimately became his primary source of income. We spent a good part of the week at church, between rehearsals and Bible study, and other religious events. One would think it would be beneficial to the psyche; but being at the church often only added to the problem of having to live up to external norms. The verbal altercations began at home and would pause at the entrance of the church doors, where we put on our church faces for hours.

When service was over, we would pick up where we left off.

Depression continued to rear its ugly face in light of the financial crisis. Work was no longer an option for me. It was the only option. Luckily, it had never been hard for me to secure work. But, after birthing an additional three children while in the marriage, the perception of my marriage changed. Hubby soon became a stay-at-home dad, usually picking up gigs that paid under the table. He was the church musician who also made money through local band gigs and auto repair. This new normal took some getting used to. Customer service was my area of expertise. I usually secured bank and utility company positions and I fared well financially.

The challenge at times was maintaining a car, which was disappointing when your hubby was a licensed mechanic. At times, I felt that was his way of controlling me and my whereabouts.

My life became a blur of a series of punched holes in the walls and drama. This time, I chose not to allow my need to be married to supersede my better judgment. When I got the cable bills with pornography charges, I knew it had to be a mistake. I called the cable company. The operator questioned me like a person on a witness stand.

"Who would be in your home, watching the television during late nights or early morning hours?"

I could only think of my husband, but it couldn't be him. The operator quickly scuffed and offered to reverse the charges. She also told me how to add a password to the cable account. After the second call to the cable company, needless to say the charges were not credited back to the account.

Pornographic movies mysteriously appeared in the house. The hubby drilled the boys about it.

"Which one of you brought these in? Which friend did you get this from?" According to him, they were not supervised in the same way that we supervised our children. Their mama did not "raise them right." Many nights, my intoxicated sleep would end abruptly as I awakened to an empty bed. After calling out into the dark hall, the hubby would appear. He was checking on a noise. Or he stepped outside to get some air. He was up checking on the children. I knew then that something wasn't right.

One day, one of the girls privately invited me to her room, on the upper bunk—where she said she woke up to her underwear pulled down. This wasn't the first time that she awakened to her underwear pulled down. It wasn't the first time that she'd been awakened by being touched on her private area by the monster. Immediately, I had a conversation with the hubby about it. He assured me that he would watch out for the boys in the night. My desire to drink diminished immediately. Therefore, both of us monitored who went where in the middle of the night. For weeks, there were no more questionable acts in the middle of the night.

But soon, the infidelity returned to the tune of me proposing marital counseling or else. By this time, we were attending a new church that offered the hubby higher pay as the musician. This pastor and his wife scheduled a date and time to meet with us. Hubby came to me before the initial appointment and said that he was willing to do counseling, but he didn't want this pastor to know everything that was going on with us. I had to stick to discussing marriage only or he would not participate. I agreed. During the meeting, his body language mimicked the meeting we had with his ex. He was uninterested and shut down. These non-verbal cues were a shock to me. I thought we were fighting for our marriage. This meeting went nowhere fast. He had nothing to say. He didn't know why he was there. The meeting was my whole idea.

At a loss for words, the pastor and his wife shared a few life experiences that they thought would help. They invited us back at any time. Things were never the same between us after that night. Hubby took up residence on the sofa in the living room. In the past, following the lead of my intuition, I made a surprise lunch visit to one of his previous jobs, confronting him and introducing myself as his wife to his female co-worker who he was entertaining. After weeks of not sleeping in the same bed and being completely cut off from intimacy and communication, my feelings of insecurity increased. I took the liberty of following him. We ended up at his friend's place and, once again, I confronted him. This resulted in me chasing after him in my car. He eventually obtained a personal protection order against me to stay away from him and his "friend." During this chaotic episode, I used my cell to call the pastor to let him know that my husband had taken up with one of the members of his church.

Pastor responded, "Psalm 15:1 says, 'A soft answer turns away wrath.'"

Excuse me? The last thing I wanted to hear was a Scripture.

"Did you hear what I said? He is cheating on me and I am over here right now!"

I repented for the things that I said to that man of God that night.

Hours after that incident, I temporarily moved my four children and myself into the home of a relative. I couldn't evict him from my family home because we were married. In a week's time, he finally moved out with his four children in tow. Our blended family was instantaneously dismantled. My four children and I returned to my family home to begin our new normal. This marital charade had lasted ten years. We managed to remain together without separation. Year eleven, we finally separated and the mourning of my marriage began. The mourning yielded a relief after a while. It felt like the sun was shining. It was as if it hadn't shined in ten years. Hubby and I agreed to disagree and we maintained a cordial relationship for the sake of the children.

Later that year, I received a call from one of the girls. The night touching had returned. I had a long talk with the girls, explaining the importance of telling the truth. I also explained the amount of trouble this would cause if they were making this up. After the second phone call of this nature, I picked the girls up from a relative's home, drove them to the seventh precinct and filed a report. Hubby always brought the children with him when he came to visit our children. The girls talked to me privately about incidents that took place in the home, which included a visit from Child Protective Services. By this time, their mom had returned from the shadows. Naturally, the children welcomed her back. She didn't regain custody of them though, even after learning of the allegations.

One day, she got word that hubby was at my home with the children. She showed up with an aluminum bat and her brother. She destroyed the hubby's car with the bat, daring him to approach her after what he had inflicted upon her children. She apologized to me for the scene in front of my home and made her exit. Eventually, there was a hearing where the girls and I were summoned to testify under oath. The charges were dropped due to not having enough evidence to prosecute. At year twelve, for reasons unknown, all four children were removed from hubby's custody and placed in foster care. At year thirteen, I managed to secure an attorney and filed for divorce. Thirteen years and five days later, our divorce was final.

The relationship between my hubby and our children was déjà vu. He went on to remarry a few months after our divorce was finalized. After multiple years, child support was never paid as ordered. Eventually, the ex-hubby came around to take the children for the weekends and summers. Praying, fasting and seeking godly wisdom, as well as intercessory prayer, was not mentioned as often as it was utilized. But these pillars were the catalysts to maintaining my sanity for thirteen long years.

This dissolution of marriage came as a shock to many because we knew how to pretend like all was well. From the outside looking in, we were a very goodlooking, young couple with children who had so much fun together. In reality, we were inexperienced, young individuals who lacked the guidance and tools required to not only enter the institution of marriage—but to maintain a marriage, procreate and raise a healthy family. We were ill-equipped to identify, control or diminish internal and external obstacles that arose. We thought we were doing what was right by seeking to marry and not committing fornication, honoring God's law.

I believe we had the desire to take the right steps, but both of us were the products of single parents. We mimicked what we thought was the process of having a spouse and family. But we didn't have married mentors or counseling to assist with learning the fundamentals. Unfortunately, the examples that we mimicked may have been another's couple normal, but not necessarily a healthy union. If I had to do it all over again, I would not had wed at the ripe age of twenty-one without any life experience and direction. Lives were forever changed. There were many lessons learned after having to endure some of the same tests multiple times. I would not have changed our separation. I don't support the idea of staying for the wellbeing of the children.

I believe our separation provided them with a foundation of happiness. It allowed them to live the rest of their childhood in flourishing, positive environments.

All of our children have reached the legal age of eighteen years old and are living their lives on their own terms. Communication between the stepchildren and I eventually diminished. Our children live in the shadow of resentment, a broken home and some predisposed mental health issues. Today, I am an advocate for my children and for therapy. This advocacy is the result of the regret of never exploring my own personal or my potential spouse's family dynamics, mental and physical health issues, family secrets and exploitations.

I have taken the time to discover who I am as an individual. I've learned to be receptive, open and fully present to my soul mate when the time presents itself. I spent many years learning my likes, dislikes, beliefs and limitations. I've spent significant time embracing therapy and establishing a personal relationship with my higher power. I am equipped with critical and logical thinking. I am now better informed on specific questions to explore to learn some of the most important parts of another's life, aspirations and purpose.

My goal and purpose are to teach from my experience and guide those who come in contact with me, whether in social connections or professional interactions. I will help others avoid some of the same pitfalls by education, empowerment and support—something I wish I had from the very start.

Straight Talk, No Chaser
SELF-REFLECTION

1. What is your life's purpose? Does this purpose or calling have the flexibility for your partner to be a part of it?

2. For better or for worse. In sickness and in health. Have these conditions of most marriage vows been defined by you and your partner?

3. Feelings can be fickle, but connectivity is important between partners. What are your thoughts on marrying for love?

4. If your marriage ended in divorce, what steps will you take to explore any unresolved issues and feelings?

5. If divorce was the result of your marriage, are you open to marriage again in the future? Why/Why not?

About the Author
➥ Patricia D. Sims

While many people try to define themselves and find their purpose in external sources, Patricia D. Sims knows firsthand that true purpose can only be unlocked from within. Pat learned early on in life that, not only were the people around her unequipped to define her self-worth, but they were also ill prepared to groom the gifts which had been divinely placed within her.

As a divorced mother of four, Pat has made it her life's mission to serve as a beacon of hope and enlightenment for anyone she comes in contact with. Her passion to positively impact the lives of others, coupled with her formal training as a mental health counselor, serves as a platform to touch lives far beyond her backyard. To further expand her reach, she founded PDSWellness, LLC, where clients receive authentic therapeutic or coaching services at an affordable rate.

Pat is adamant about measuring her success by the impact she leaves on the hearts of men and women that can't easily be erased. For more information, visit www.pdswellness.com or email PDSWellness@gmail.com.

The Perfect Wife for the New Man
by Robin Burrus

Through the many trials and tribulations in my marriage, I've always known that my husband was an intricate part of my testimony. The part I didn't know was whether or not he would be in my life when it was time to share that testimony. Would he be my husband or my ex-husband once the marriage testimony manifested? I didn't struggle with whether or not we would be together. I struggled with knowing if we would actually be together *forever*.

Initially, I married because I was young and excited. I loved him and I was *chosen*. I was excited about the wedding and excited to start a life on "grown woman status" as I saw it. Growing up, the guys never chose me. So, not only did I get a good man, but he also looked good. He was saved and went to church, and he wanted *me*. I was his *one*.

People marry for various reasons. While the main reason should be love, for many, that's not the case. When I was a teenager, I made a vow to myself that I didn't want to date. I witnessed too many people hop from one boyfriend or girlfriend to the next. I planned to meet a guy I could grow up and old with. While I had my fair share of promiscuity as a teen, I only had two boyfriends. The second boyfriend became my husband. I met him in December of 2004. For a young girl with low self-esteem, the one who the guys never chose, I was looking good the day we met.

Proverbs 12:4 (NIV) says, *A wife of noble character is her husband's crown, but a disgraceful wife is like decay in his bones.*

Dating was amazing! He introduced me to so many things. We attended church almost every week. He ran the audio system in the church and tried his best to live a life that was pleasing in God's sight. After church each week, he took me to eat.

We talked on the phone for hours, but we always wanted to be together. At the time, I lived on the westside of Detroit. He'd travel west from the eastside just for us to sit in the car and listen to gospel music. We played our favorite song over and over again. At one point, I moved in with my best friend so that I could go to school from her house and be closer to him. I was going through a lot at home a few months prior, so I moved out of my mother's house at the age of 17.

Valentine's Day was two months after we started dating. I came home to my best friend's house to find a bouquet of roses, a bear and a card that seemed to be written by the Lord himself. To this day, my husband still picks out the best cards. The card was a number one, representing our first Valentine's Day together. My eyes melt at the thought even now.

He was always full of surprises. He often picked me up from work and, after driving a few minutes, would tell me to open the glove box. In the glove box would be single roses in different colors, for different reasons. He bought me beautiful outfits to wear on our date nights. He was perfect! He was older than me by a little over two years. How could he be so young, but so romantic? Where did he get this from and how did he know of some of the places he took me?

Literally, three months into dating, he got my name tattooed on his arm. That was huge! I was shocked, excited and nervous at the same time. What did it mean? A tattoo is permanent. This was my first *real* relationship. This had to mean he really liked me and was digging me, right? Someone was really choosing *me*. There were some interesting days, but the good outweighed the bad. I was enjoying myself.

After two years of dating, he proposed to me at his cousin's baby shower in front of all of his family and church friends. We married a few months later.

Marriage is beautiful. Marriage is cute. Someone once said, "Everyone wants to be a princess for a day." I realized I wasn't ready for the marriage—*after the wedding*. I struggled with miscarriages while we dated. A relative once told me, "Don't worry. It'll happen in God's timing." They were right. One month after my wedding, I found out I was two months pregnant. For the next three years, I had a baby annually. We didn't waste time. At first, I was ashamed for having my children back to back, until I realized they would grow up together since they were close in age. My mother-in-love and I clashed because she knew it was too much for me at one time, but I didn't understand her point of view.

Remember that the enemy comes to steal, kill and destroy. He wants to ruin everything, to go against God's plans for our lives. If he can end a marriage, he'll leave two people broken. If he can end a marriage with children, he can ruin their lives at a young age. He can ruin the dynamics of family. It doesn't give children anything to look forward to when it comes to marriage, so they are set up for failure.

My husband would not allow us to argue in front of the children. One day, I was yelling and fussing when our children were younger. He took the children and walked away. That day, I learned that arguing in front of the children was out of the question.

The Shoes

We fought about everything. One day, I read *The Power of a Praying Wife* by Stormie Omartian. The book talked about how women kept nagging about the same thing instead of changing their outlook and perspective. During this time, I remember my husband would take his shoes off and set them right next to the closet as opposed to *in the closet*. I worked hard to keep a clean house with three babies, so I didn't want to fight with the only other adult in the house. Reading that part in the book changed my life. Instead of nagging and irritating myself and him, I just put the shoes in the closet. It may seem small or stupid, but I was at peace. I got rid of the attitude and he didn't have to hear my mouth, murmuring and complaining. It was that simple. Just put the shoes up.

Don't Blame/Own Your Own Actions

Recently, I realized that my husband hated me. In his eyes, I thought I was perfect. While he was wrong, I can see his point of view. Most of the time, our communication was filled with miscommunication. We misinterpreted one another most of the time. While he thought I felt I could do no wrong, I always tried to see both sides of the issue.

One week, my husband refused to talk to me until we got help. We literally didn't communicate until we went to a marriage counselor. We met with her a few times and I learned a lot quickly. One time, she made us sit, facing each other, knee to knee. She told me to say whatever I wanted to say to him. My conversation was filled with a series of, "You always ... blah, blah, blah. You do this. You do that. You, you, you, you, you!"

When my time was up, she said, "Now it's your turn."

He said, "I don't have anything to say."

I was livid. He decided when he wanted to talk and when he didn't. He got to walk away when he wanted to. She then taught me all about the "I" statements. I needed to learn how to use the word "I" instead of "you." As I look back now, I was attacking him on a regular basis. He was living a miserable life. He was the blame for everything and I was perfect. This was definitely grounds for divorce ... or someone ending up in a body bag.

On another occasion, we went to marriage counseling at our church. We took the Five Love Languages quiz, which identifies the language in which you give and receive emotional love. Written by Gary Chapman, the book's theory believes that once you identify and learn your mate's love language, it's the key to a long-lasting and loving marriage. The five love languages consist of: receiving gifts, quality time, words of affirmation, acts of service and personal touch. Ironically, words of affirmation were both of our number one love languages. My husband did not agree and suggested that there was something wrong with the results. I, on the other hand, understood it totally.

Most women look at males as masculine beings. But, they're still human. Their egos need to be stroked. They need to be encouraged. However, most women don't look at those needs as being a man's number one love language. It may not be every male, but I'm sure it's one of their top two. I realized that my husband actually needed to be affirmed by my words when, in fact, all I was doing was bashing and blaming him. But, in his mind, I was perfect. Our marriage was unhealthy for so many years.

Proverbs 27:15-16 (MSG) says, *A nagging spouse is like the drip, drip, drip of a leaky faucet; You can't turn it off, and you can't get away from it.*

Mental health is real. My husband faced some trying times from the inside out. Can you imagine not having control of your mind? Can you imagine hating the person you're with? Can you imagine hating to come home because you will have to hear someone's mouth? My husband didn't have to imagine it.

He lived it.

I am a very talkative person and I want to talk about *everything*. My husband is the opposite. I struggled with that because I felt like he held the power of when we could talk and when we couldn't. If he didn't want to talk about something, we couldn't. But when he did want to talk, we better had talked right then and there. That is how I felt at the counseling session. He decided he was done and wouldn't respond to my conversation. Why should he have responded though? He was being attacked—daily.

For years, I made statements like, "This is your world. However you want it is how it has to be. Only your way counts and nothing else matters." What I was missing was that there was time for talking, and there was a time to not talk. You should never force a situation when the time is not right. During our dating and early days of marriage, very seasoned women told me to, "Choose my battles."

If only I would have actually understood what they meant. Everything does not have to be a conversation. Everything does not have to be my way. My way of understanding is not the only way of understanding.

When your man is ready to talk, *you* be ready. Allow him to speak because most of the time, men don't want to talk. When men take the time to actually talk, it's usually because they need to get something out. This is not a time for us to interrupt but a time to solely listen.

From experience, I recommend only giving feedback or advice if asked. In my marriage, my husband found it disrespectful for me to cut him off or interrupt with my example or concern of the issue. He said that I only wanted to talk but never wanted to listen. It was rude that he would listen to me for what seemed like all the time but as soon as he was ready to talk, I didn't give him the chance. He felt like I was uninterested in his conversation and only wanted to tell him about me. This could be a form of rejection. Have you ever found yourself in this predicament? If this area is violated, it's a form of rejection. No one takes rejection well, so we must be careful how we respond to others.

James 1:19 (NIV) says, *Understand this, my dear brothers and sisters: You must all be quick to listen, slow to speak, and slow to get angry.*

Rejection

"For too many people the fear of rejection and the desire for acceptance are the main motivating forces for all actions in their lives. It plays a part in their choices concerning their education, career direction, work behavior, achievement level, interpersonal and marital relationships, family and community life, and the ways in which they spend leisure time. The person who operates out of a fear of rejection all too often ends up pushing away the very friends, family, and helpers who care the most. The pulling away of these caring ones appears to be rejection, and the vicious cycle goes on with negative results."[1]

---

1 Retrieved July 8, 2018, from PsychologistAnywhereAnytime.com website: http://www.psychologistanywhereanytime.com/relationships_psychologist/psychologist_rejection.htm.

"Emotional rejection is the feeling a person experiences when disappointed about not achieving something desired. It is commonly experienced in a quest of emotional relations, such as among romantic couples, in social and group settings, or in the professional world in relation to advancement. The act of rejection can make the person experiencing it undergo a sudden drop in positive emotion. This is displayed as something ranging from a vague disappointment, sadness, and depression to anxiety, phobic behavior, or even stalking or forcibly abducting the rejecting person."

One day, I found myself faced with a hurt man and a rifle in our bedroom. This was it. I felt sick to my stomach. I was standing in our room at the top of the stairs thinking, *"Will I survive? God, is this it? What about all the kids downstairs? Can I run and get away? How will I get away?"*

During this time, there were many news reports of men killing women. Women were found cut up in their garages. There was a murder spirit going around. The culprits were the husbands or boyfriends of these women. Women ranged in age from young to old. Celebrity couples, who, to the outside world appeared to be doing great, were also affected. We were not good. The enemy was clearly in control. My husband is not *crazy*, but he did lose control of his mind at one point.

Have you ever hated someone so bad that you thought of hurting them? I've felt this way, so I can't blame him. We were stressed, and our marriage was unhealthy.

Mental Illness

1. Mental illnesses can affect people of any age, race, religion or income. It is a medical condition that disrupts a person's thinking, feeling, mood and ability to relate to others and daily functioning.

2. Serious mental illnesses include: major depression, schizophrenia, bipolar disorder, obsessive compulsive disorder (OCD), panic disorder, post-traumatic stress disorder (PTSD) and borderline personality disorder.

3. Depression is the leading cause of disability worldwide.[2]

Scriptures to Cope with Mental Illness

- ✓ 1 Peter 5:7: *Casting all your anxiety on Him, because He cares for you.*

- ✓ John 14:27: *Peace I leave with you; My peace I give to you; not as the world gives do I give to you. Do not let your heart be troubled, nor let it be fearful.*

- ✓ Matthew 6:34: *So do not worry about tomorrow; for tomorrow will care for itself. Each day has enough trouble of its own.*

- ✓ Ephesians 4:23: *... And that you be renewed in the spirit of your mind.*

---

[2] NIH. "Any Mental Illness (AMI) Among U.S. Adults." National Institute of Mental Health. Accessed October 31, 2016.

When situations become unhealthy like these my husband and I experienced, seek help immediately. He was able to shake that demon quickly. Of course, I lived in fear for a while because I didn't know if it would rise back up again. However, I also knew when a situation was going too far and when to back off. I knew when I shouldn't provoke it anymore. This is not considered stepping down or being submissive. This is an act of having knowledge and wisdom.

My husband asked me a question one day concerning an uncomfortable situation. It was a past concern, but my answer was one that I learned from him. Early on in the marriage, he always asked me if the bad outweighed the good. Interestingly, I felt like the bad did outweigh the good now. Our marriage was so bad that it was hard for me to remember the good things. I felt like we were roommates. The bad did outweigh the good, but it hit me right there.

This marriage really has been a huge misunderstanding, and we are now reversing it.

I consider myself to be a nurturer. I am an assistant by nature, and I want to improve any area I'm a part of. As my mother-in-love says, "I can do all things." Unfortunately, I know now that I *can't* do all things, but I really did used to try to. I could be an assistant for life because I have no desire to be in the forefront. I just want to get the job done to satisfy God and my soul. I just want to help people. I want to help, but I realized in my helping that I was complicating my husband's life more. My husband felt that he was the blame for everything, and I was an angel who could do no wrong. Nine times out of ten, I thought that my ideas were the best ideas. I rarely gave him a chance to "be a man."

My mother-in-love used to say, "Don't put too much on his plate!" I despised her for that. He's grown and she needed to get a life! Oh, how I should've listened. I didn't get it! I can multitask and literally manage a million things at once, but my husband cannot. My brain can balance a million moving pieces while he's still trying to get in the game. All I wanted to do was *help* him because I knew I could think faster. I wasn't saying that he was dumb, but I've learned that it takes him more time to process things. My intentions are always good; but was I actually making the situation worse?

Genesis 2:18-22 (BSB) says, *The Lord God said, "It is not good for the man to be alone. I will make him a suitable helper." Now the Lord God formed out of the ground all the beasts of the field and all the birds of the air. He brought them to the man to see what he would name them and whatever the man called each living creature, that was its name. So, the man gave names to all the livestock, the birds of the air and all the beasts of the field. But for Adam no suitable helper could be found. So, the Lord God caused the man to fall into a deep sleep; and while he was sleeping, he took one of the man's ribs and closed up the place with flesh. Then the Lord God made a woman from the rib he had taken out of the man and brought her to the man.*

Wives refer to themselves in different forms. Some consider themselves to be a helpmate while others consider themselves to be a helpmeet. To me it's tomato (toe-may-toe) Tomato (toe-mah-toe); an unimportant difference; but since people want to use it, I've created my own version. For years, I didn't know the difference. After searching the internet and Scriptures for both words, I realized the Scripture comes up under "help meet," meaning a suitable helper for him (Adam) and the Scripture ends. That could mean anything. It could have meant someone to help him with the animals. When you search the definition of "helpmate," it says a companion and helper. I now consider myself to be a helpmate (companion) who is designed to help meet (helper in situations) the needs of my husband. I choose to use both aspects or versions.

Communication

Communication is one of the main reasons people divorce. As much as we tried to get the other person to do so, I didn't hear him and my husband didn't hear me. Can you talk to your spouse? Of course you can. Get some tips. Take a deep breath and *listen*.

I would later learn that my husband would have wonderful, life-changing conversations with other women. But he was supposed to. That's how the enemy works. The enemy wanted to destroy us by making the grass look greener on the other side for him. This is where you have to watch for barriers. I realized I didn't have a chance to communicate with him for many years. I didn't stand a chance. The first time I said anything he didn't like, or something he didn't agree with, he thought about how much easier this conversation would be with another woman. This was all a plan of the enemy though.

We had simple misunderstandings. It's so hard to be in a relationship when you are always misunderstood. Communication is not easy. It takes work and time to perfect it.

While writing this piece, I asked my husband for forty dollars. He had $140. Yet, he had plans for the money. I wanted to do something extra, but it was for the children. It stressed him out. Here I was, asking for money when he thought I knew the plans he had for the money. I didn't. In my mind, it was easy for him to just say, "No." We could've simply moved right along. However, in his mind, I was adding pressure and stress.

Women are considered to be the helpmeet, but in actuality, our husbands are the same for us. Our husbands are there to meet our needs and be the savior to our requests.

My husband mentioned a few other things that I blurted off the top of my head as ideas. I was just talking and many of the things were long-term goals. What I didn't realize was that he was *actually* paying attention to me. Who knew that he was analyzing me and trying to plan a solution to the many ideas that drift in my head? I needed to slow down. I didn't realize the simple things I did could cause stress to my honey. Ladies, while our intentions are good, we don't realize how our actions affect others. Be careful and understand the personalities of the people around you.

> *If you both can't work toward the change,*
> *one of you must.*

Proverbs 18:22 (NIV) says, *He who finds a wife finds what is good and receives favor from the LORD.*

No matter what, pray. Many times, praying will be the last thing you want to do, but you must. My husband and I were trying to do marriage on our own terms. We only sought God when we hit rock bottom.

> *If God is faithful to us, then surely,*
> *we can be faithful to our spouses.*
> *We need to forgive and dismiss the faults.*

I've been married for eleven years. For ten years and ten months, I was mentally abused. Not on purpose but as a defense to all my husband was going through with me. Since I already had low self-esteem before I met my husband, things didn't get better because I got married. I always feared that the light-skinned, thick girl would take my husband. I always felt like he regretted marrying me. He didn't show me affection at all. I can't even remember the good times we had. Often, I questioned myself, "Was *it* ever good? When did we have sex? Where did the kids come from? Did we talk in the beginning?" That's how bad things were. The bad totally outweighed the good.

One day, one of our close friends brought it to his attention. Right in front of me, our friends pointed out to him that they'd never seen him show me affection. Wow, it wasn't just me. Other people noticed. This was so embarrassing. It didn't help that I thought he was ashamed or embarrassed of me either. It's simple to please me. I don't need much. It's the thought that counts. Our friends were too lovey-dovey for me, but I still needed something. *Anything.* Truth is, I wasn't getting it in private or in public.

Watch Out Now

There was a gentleman at work who was very pleasing to the eye. He seemed quiet and shy, but he was cool. We saw one another in passing. But one day after he left, he called to tell me how beautiful I was to him. He talked about the way the sun shined on my skin and how he loved to see me coming. This, of course, was not the attention I was used to receiving. He knew I was married, but he just wanted to "kick it." Not wanting to be rude or hurt his feelings, I said "I'm pretty good and we're cool." We saw one another often, so I didn't want to make things awkward. I was good on having conversations with him. He was still a nice gentleman.

Unfortunately, I fed into it. Now that I knew someone was watching me, and paying me close attention, I brushed my hair a little more. I straightened every wrinkle in my clothes. I oiled my legs more often. I even glossed my lips right before we would pass each other.

Cheating isn't always kissing, touching or flirting. If you have to delete your text messages so your partner won't see them, you're already there.
–Unknown

Someone was paying attention to me. Someone was giving me something that I was not used to receiving. I was always scared to cheat. Cheating when you're married is considered adultery. I feared breaking the covenant I made before the Lord more than I did my husband. I just knew that I would be punished right away. It went against everything I ever was. Everything I respected.

Watch the Company You Keep

I knew some people who had affairs. Because of that, I found myself asking many questions: *How did you do it? When did you have time? Where did you meet?* I asked so many questions that I believe the enemy used those things to plant seeds in my head. Someone once told me, "You will make time." And that I did.

I always held a position as a receptionist, administrative assistant or executive assistant. Working at the front desk, I hated taking a lunch. It's obvious when you're away and it always seemed so hard to get back into the groove of things when you return. I had an hour lunch, so I found myself visiting this particular gentleman during my lunch often. I told my husband I was staying late for projects or going in early to work just to make sure I spent time with this gentleman. Small conversations eventually lead to infidelity.

A mistake is an accident. Cheating and lying are not mistakes; they are intentional choices.
–Unknown

I committed adultery in 2015. Eight years into my marriage, this went against everything in me. I thought it was an amazing decision at the time. This man gave me everything I was missing, or so I thought. There was both an emotional and physical connection. He fed my mind, body and soul everything I was lacking.

> *Most people cheat because they're paying more attention to what they're missing than what they have.*
> –Unknown

Remember, the enemy comes to kill, steal and destroy. He wanted to destroy my marriage from the onset. How dare two young people, who love the Lord, get married and start a family! How dare they try to live a happy life and raise a godly family! Did we think we could raise these wonderful children with no mishaps? Was it realistic to think that evil wouldn't try to tear their minds up, too? The enemy was out for us. At the time, though, we were too blind and dumb to see it.

I literally pictured myself starting a new life with the other man. I was the happiest I had ever been in a long time. But, I found myself being increasingly ruder to my husband. I didn't care about anything my husband was talking about or anything he was doing. I didn't care if he was coming or going. I had mentally planned my new life with a new man. I knew my children couldn't come with me, so I saw myself as one of those mothers who paid child support to their ex-husbands. My husband wouldn't dare allow his children to leave his side. I could go, but they had to stay.

I thought about everything I would do differently with the new man that I had not, could not, or would not do with my husband. I was going to be the perfect wife for the next man! I knew where I'd made mistakes and I figured I could be the woman of someone else's dreams since I wasn't the woman of my husband's dreams. I know I'm a great woman and my husband was going to regret the day he ever did any wrong by me once he saw how happy I was with my new man.

Our marriage may have seemed horrible, but the crazy part was that it had come a long way. It was just bipolar to us. We had extremely high highs and very low lows. When we were up, everything was good. When we were not, things were an absolute nightmare.

When I asked the gentleman who I was involved with, who had one child, his short-term and long-term goals, I thought about the job he had at the time. I was trying to determine if there was opportunity for growth there for him. He was also a felon and it was usually hard for felons to find good paying jobs. He didn't have a real career. I asked him about his personal dreams and goals. Did he want more kids? I asked about his family and I was smart enough to even ask him about his credit score. I loved my current in-laws, so I needed to know if I was going to be a part of another great family.

However, his answers didn't sit right with me.

I stopped having conversations with those people who had previously committed adultery. Those conversations made it worse every time. My spirit would tell me to get out of the mess I was in, but I continued to be intrigued by the spice of my friends' infidelity. I needed to separate myself. But my time with this man was going so well that I couldn't let it go. I was falling more and more for this man.

I was falling alright, and fast. I wasn't even sure what or who I was falling for.

When the Holy Spirit moves, you abide. The Lord offered me many ways of escape, but I chose not to. Subsequently, the Lord set me up in a three-day time span where I received a call for an interview for a job I didn't apply for. I received an offer, but I declined because it didn't seem worth the change. The next offer I received was $8,000 more than my current salary. The offers didn't stop there. Because I still had to get my children to school, the job offer came with the stipulation of, "What's a good time for you to start after you drop your children off?"

If this wasn't a way of escape, I don't know what is.

The Lord removed me from that situation because He knew I was too dumb to remove myself. I knew it was Him though, and I acknowledged it right away. I was still in communication with the gentleman a little after my career change, but I drifted further away slowly but surely. I didn't want to block his number because I still wanted to know when he was thinking of me. Shortly thereafter, I realized that there was no sense in keeping that up because it would lead to more temptation. I blocked the number and didn't look back. That was a wrap! Three months of infidelity, a wrecked brain and a heart filled with shame. It crushed my soul. It crushed my very being and all I stood for. I now lived with a secret that ate away at me every day.

Yet, I hated my husband. I regretted my children. I hated the day I met him, our first date and the day he was ever born. He'd hurt me to my core. He called me fat, black and ugly many times. He hated me. He regretted marrying me and he was stuck.

We were stuck. These were all the thoughts I had in my head. Yet, I chose to stay because I don't find faults in other people. People want to blame others for their misery, but I beg to differ. We have control over our feelings and emotions. My husband was not at fault or the blame for my misery. *We were.* We both operated from a different point of view. Instead of marrying and becoming one, we were still individuals living like individuals. We didn't listen to the other person.

Ephesians 6:12 (KJV) says, *For we wrestle not against flesh and blood, but against principalities, against powers, against the rulers of the darkness of this world, against spiritual wickedness in high places.*

While I don't think my husband meant to say many things that he said over time, in the moment, that's what he needed to say. Those were the things that made him feel better. It takes a strong woman to admit that, recognize it and ignore that demon for what it is.

My infidelity tore me to pieces. I always hoped I'd catch him cheating so that I'd find relief.

It didn't happen that way. Things shifted.

Our marriage became *different*. We communicated well for the first time in ten years and ten months. We heard one another. We understood each other. And when we didn't, we took great strides to make things make sense until the other person understood. At this point, I learned that we were both at our wit's end. He had given up and so had I. Neither one of us actually *wanted* to give up. We wanted to be the long-lasting family and marriage we heard of, but never really witnessed. We wanted to be the example we heard of for our children.

I prayed for the Lord to give me the opportune time to come clean about my infidelity. He did just that.

"Have you cheated on me?" he asked.

I balled my eyes out before I could respond. I knew it was time. It went smoothly, not because he was so understanding, but because he had been cheating, too, since the beginning of the marriage. He'd spent the entire ten years of our marriage interacting with different people. I had cheated for three months with one guy. I didn't care how many women he had been with, when, where or how. I was just relieved and knew that it was a breakthrough moment for our marriage.

We had both been praying for a change; this time for real. I believe that our confessions to one another allowed us to release built up tensions. Our infidelity was a major stronghold to the marriage and we were now released. Our communication was at an all-time high. We now practiced patience and love when dealing with one another.

It has been amazing ever since.

I'm sure you're wondering how in the hell I could move on. Remember, I said I wanted to marry young and grow old with the person. It's happening. It has happened. They say that men are from Mars and women are from Venus, meaning we have two totally different ways of thinking. During those miserable years, I held on because I noticed that it wasn't just us. We weren't the only couple in the planet going through challenges. I've read books, watched seminars, went to counseling and attended a marriage boot camp all to find out that it wasn't *just us*. It was *all* men and women. Ninety percent of marriages have the same issues: communication, finances and infidelity. People of all nationalities, demographics and denominations have the same issues. We just can't see it when we're in the midst of going through the process.

> *If you want it to last, it will.*
> *If you want it to end, it can!*
> –Me

While my marriage may seem like it was doomed from the beginning, it has actually come a long way. Our marriage was bipolar, though. We were either on cloud nine or at rock bottom. There never seemed to be an in-between phase. For 90% of it, I felt like we were just roommates. We just stuck it out.

Of course, the feminine side of me kicked in a few days later and I wanted to know all the details. Unfortunately, the world is more accepting of men cheating. But when a woman cheats, it's the end of the world. My husband was hurt and I didn't care. I'm still processing the fact that I had a three-month-long affair, while my husband was involved with various women for over ten years. I did, however, thank my husband for keeping me covered in the midst of his cheating. I was never humiliated! I never had to deal with women calling my phone, coming to my house, blasting him on social media or popping up with a baby. To me, this was important! They say, "hurt people hurt people." My husband was hurt and so was I. He has his own reasons. He has his own thoughts. He has his own feelings. We married young, which many considered to be a mistake. But we've made it this far.

Overall, I've realized that it's not just him and I. It's not his fault. It's not my fault. Men and women are just different. When someone is ready to get married, they have to become one with another individual, which is not as easy as it seems. It takes love, patience, kindness, understanding and a whole lot of prayer.

I ran across an article that dated back to the 1950s, *Tips to Look After Your Husband from a Home Economics Book*. The chapter titles included: Have Dinner Ready, Prepare Yourself, Prepare the Children, Minimize All Noise, Make Him Comfortable, Listen to Him, Make the Evening His and more.

I screenshot a picture of the article from a Facebook post, but have thought very deeply about it. I knew that many women would have a lot to say against it. One thing it made me see is the women back then. It seemed as if they never faced divorce. Women in older days lived on through thick and thin. Divorce didn't seem like an option for them. You didn't hear about their husbands being unsatisfied or their nagging natures. This seemed to be something new in age. Back in these times, women seemed to keep their husbands with little issues compared to the concerns our relationships face today.

Now more than ever, I'm clear that the woman sets the tone for the household. Be careful of the tone that you present in your home. Our children are affected by our tone. We are affected. But more importantly, we affect our husbands.

Today, I consider myself to be the perfect wife for the "new" man. I know you began reading thinking I must've been talking about another man and it was almost true. However, I'm the perfect wife for "my" *new* man. I have a totally different husband from the one I married eleven years ago. I have a totally different husband than the one I was with even a year ago. I love my marriage and the space we are in. I'm a new woman and my husband is a new man.

Straight Talk, No Chaser
SELF-REFLECTION

1. What does fighting for your marriage look like at this point?

   _____
   _____

2. What part of your marital problems do you take responsibility for?

   _____
   _____

3. In what ways can you relinquish control and let your husband lead the family and marriage?

   _____
   _____

4. How do you and your mate feel about marriage counseling, seminars, workshops or even reading marriage books together?

   _____
   _____

About the Author
➥ Robin Burrus

She was always chosen last. As a young girl, Robin was always teased by peers and had low self-esteem. She never had a good example of what a godly marriage looked like or what it should entail. When she married her second boyfriend, all she knew was that it was totally different from what she had previously known.

Married at the age of 20 after only dating for two years, Robin is now thriving in a once dying marriage. In the midst of the threat of divorce, mental illness, infidelity and hatred, her marriage is now at an all-time high. Robin seeks to inspire women who are married or desiring marriage to overcome the challenges they are sure to face. She believes that many marital mishaps can be avoided, but only by those who are willing to do the work.

Blinded by Love
by Ortavia McClain

After being in an eight-year relationship with someone who cheated on me after my right femur fracture, I decided to just be single. I cried myself to sleep many nights. I questioned myself, *"What was I doing wrong in the relationship? Why did I attract cheating men?"* I was loyal and faithful during the eight years we were together. After the break-up, I talked to an ex on the phone about my situation. He tried to console me with his conversation and his presence.

I knew my heart was not healed from my relationship, but the consolation of another man made me feel like I could block out the hurt and pain while he was there. Once he left, the pain came back. I didn't want to be with my ex; I just wanted to be comforted.

My birthday was approaching in a couple of months and I didn't have any plans. I just wanted to stay home and spend my birthday with my kids—up until my best friend offered to take me out for my birthday. Even though I really didn't want to go, my best friend insisted. She thought it would cheer me up. She thought it would take my mind off my pain and help me heal. She also was seeing a guy who she wanted me to meet. He had a single friend, as well. They were meeting at the bar and he was bringing his single friend along.

"I don't know, girl. He probably got a whole lot of kids and different baby mommas," I said. "He probably doesn't have a job and he's probably broke. I have enough kids to take care of! I'm not trying to take care of nobody else's kids!"

"Girl, he's cute and he got money!" she said, encouraging me to go despite my efforts to decline. "You can find out about the kids when you meet him."

"Okay. I'll go and see. But you better be right!"

Blue and Gold

I got dressed and we met another friend at the neighborhood bar called The Blue and Gold. When I walked in, my friends were already there. I saw a lot of people I knew from the neighborhood and started mingling. While I was mingling in the bar, *he* was checking me out from head to toe.

Politely, my best friend said, "Come on, Tay. Let me introduce you to my friend and his friend."

As we were opening up for introductions, I started sneezing.

He greeted me with, "Bless you! Are you okay?"

"Yes. It's just my sinuses."

After we were officially introduced to each other, my friend and her friend went over to the bar, leaving us standing near the dance floor.

He said, "Happy birthday! What do you want to drink?"

I ordered a drink and he got a beer. I really wasn't a drinker at the time. I kept that one drink the whole time I was there. As we talked, he was very polite. He always said, "Yes, ma'am."

"So, how long have you been single?" I started in on him. "How many kids you have? Where do you work?"

"Am I applying for a job?"

"Maybe," I said as we both laughed. He made me feel special. He had a sense of humor and he was a gentleman. I was wearing a pair of dark brown leggings with a sheer orange and dark brown blouse. He had on blue jeans with the jacket to match. I started sneezing again. He took his jacket off and put it around my shoulders.

"This may help with your sneezing," he said.

As the night winded down, the DJ said, "Last call for alcohol."

"You want another drink or are you ready to go?" he asked. Before I could answer, he asked, "Can I take you to breakfast? I don't want our conversation to end."

I accepted his offer. We headed out to the parking lot and, by the time we got to my car, he said, "I have to ride with you. I didn't drive to the bar."

I was hesitant at first, but I blocked that out because I wanted to know more about him. He made me feel so special.

"So, where do you want to go eat?" he asked.

"Well, the only thing that's open is Coney Island and IHOP."

We went to IHOP.

"Do you know what you want to eat?" he asked. "You can have whatever you want."

"Thank you," I said as the waitress came to take our order. When the waitress left, we resumed our conversation. Five minutes into our conversation, his pager went off. He looked at the number and ignored it. By the time our food came, his pager went off again. I was starting to feel uneasy.

"Are you going to answer that?"

"No. It's nobody," he reassured me. His pager went off again.

"Is that your woman?"

"I told you I don't have a woman. How can I be here with you this late and have a woman at home?"

"Oh, it can be done!"

"I'm about to handle this right now," he said, excusing himself from the table. He went to the phone booth. He came back within five minutes.

"Now, that situation is handled and everything that I've told you thus far is the truth."

Eventually, he told me that was his daughter's mother blowing up his pager.

"Are you still seeing each other?" I asked boldly.

"No! She calls from time to time to get a bag of weed. That's all. Now that I've met you, all I want is you."

Home Sweet Home

The next morning, I woke up with this man in my bed. My emotions were all over the place. I felt stupid. My sister brought my kids home and I knew they were going to see this man.

I thought to myself, *"What are they going to say? What are they going to think?"* Instantly, I said to myself, "This is my life. I'm grown and I'm the mother."

I introduced the kids to him and, in the beginning, everything and everyone was good. After he officially moved in, we became a family. It was home sweet home.

He used my car to make his runs from the eastside to the westside of Detroit at least twice a week. He paid the bills and cooked, while I worked and shopped.

As we moved forward in our relationship, we started having problems. He started coming home later. His pager was ringing at all times of the night. Immediately, I thought he was cheating. We got into a big argument one night about the pager, which caused him to throw the pager up against the wall to keep me from thinking that the alerts were from another woman.

I let it go.

After being in a relationship for over a year, he asked me to marry him and, of course, I accepted his proposal. I was happy and excited to become his wife. I immediately envisioned how I wanted my wedding day. Before we could get to the altar though, all those late nights out, going to the westside and bringing home money, was just the beginning of more heartache and struggle for me. While he was out in the streets making money, the Feds were watching him. They were building a case against him and his friend.

It was 10:30 a.m. on a Wednesday when the house phone rang. We were upstairs in the bed asleep, and my daughter and niece were in the bedroom downstairs asleep. He answered the phone, but the other person on the line did not say anything.

He hung up. Ten minutes later, the phone rang again.

The person on the other end told him, "Get up and out of the bed now!"

By the time he jumped up and answered the phone, we heard a loud noise. The Feds had kicked in our front door. They were already in the house, with their guns drawn, heading up the stairs. I have never been so frightened in my life! My first instinct was to worry about my daughter and niece waking up to see the police over them with guns drawn. There were at least four federal agents in the house.

"Who's all in the house?" they hollered out.

"It's just us and the girls are in the bedroom downstairs!" I yelled to them.

They ordered my fiancé to put on pants and a shirt before they handcuffed him.

"Ma'am, we're taking him in for some questioning. He will be out sometime later this evening," they told me.

I was scared, to say the least. I was in shock and crying hysterically. I took the girls with me to work on the midnight shift that Tuesday night. Thank God it was Bring Your Child to Work Day. After agents questioned him for hours, they released him and I went to pick him up.

"It's got to be me or them streets because I can't go through nothing like this ever again!" I told him.

He promised me he was done with that lifestyle. He even went to the temporary agency to look for work. Three months later, he had to appear in court for drug possession and money laundering. The judge sentenced him to 36 months in a federal prison. They gave him the opportunity to turn himself in to the facility in Wisconsin approximately four months after his sentence.

When we got home from court, he was silent. He didn't want to talk much for the remainder of the day. He'd never been to prison before and he was also concerned about what I was going to do.

"We have to talk about our future because being silent is not going to change what you heard this morning," I said. I'd already told him before we went to court that if he got five years, I was not going to wait. That wouldn't be fair to me and the kids. Since he was sentenced to only serve 36 months, he knew I would still be here, waiting for him. We would get through this together.

He wanted to get married right away, but I wanted a big wedding. I didn't want to get married at the court. As time got closer to him leaving, we tried to spend a lot of time together. He even stopped all communication with his friend, who received twice as much prison time as he did. When it was time for him to turn himself in, we drove to Wisconsin the day before and stayed with my family. Therefore, it wouldn't be a hardship on me when I went to visit him.

The next morning, we headed to the prison where he would spend the next three years of his life. My life with the kids went on without him, but he called twice a day and we wrote each other. I also went to see him every three months. The last year he was there, I started planning our wedding. When he got released, he had to go to the work release program (halfway house) for two months. He was allowed to be out for eight hours during the week, and he was allowed to come home on weekends. However, he always had to answer the phone whenever the Department of Corrections called.

On the day we married in August, we had the house phone transferred to his cell phone so he wouldn't miss the call when Department of Corrections did phone check. After his 6 p.m. call, we partied at our reception until 11:30 p.m. We went home as husband and wife. After doing time, it was clear he was a different person, though. He was angry for no reason or he always fussed at the kids. We argued about bills, the kids, and him finding a job (or lack thereof). While he was locked up, I found his father (whom he said was deceased) and his sister (who lived out of state, but was moving to Detroit soon). He met with his father and they strengthened their father/son relationship once he started working at his box company.

While I knew my husband was good friends with many of the employees, he started picking up a certain female employee for work. I didn't find out about this until his pager went off with a message from her asking him whether or not he was going to pick her up in the morning. I was furious! He's a married man, not her chauffeur! Once I went up to his job to let her know that he would no longer be picking her up or dropping her off, he and I got into a bigger argument. This young lady made sure she let his father know that I had made my presence known.

Shortly after that altercation, my father-in-law's business declined and he started laying off employees. My husband ended up working for Faygo as a merchandiser, due to the help of my brother-in-law. I was working for a hand surgeon. We considered selling our house and moving out of the neighborhood, which was rapidly declining. I wanted to give my kids a better opportunity, educationally and socially.

Once we sold our home, we moved to Westland. It was a challenge because of the long drive back and forth to the city for work and for the kids to attend school. I decided to put my youngest three kids in school near our new home. Soon, I lost my job because I was late too many times. My husband's job ended, as well. Eventually, we were no longer able to pay the mortgage and we lost the house.

I went into a deep depression. After spending too much money and losing a home, my marriage was hanging on by a thread. My husband shut down and our communication was minimal. I prayed to God and asked Him to get me through this hard time. I wanted God to show me what I needed to do. We reached out to family and friends for financial support, and we were able to move into a three-bedroom apartment. I got a job downriver as a medical receptionist and my husband started working at an apartment complex in Westland, four miles away from where we lived.

We were down to one car because my husband had an accident in his car leaving church one night after Bible study. I dropped him off at work in the mornings and then went to work. He'd have to sit for an hour daily until I picked him up. This went on for three months. When we got home, he always sat for hours, watching TV or talking on the phone to his sister. We went weeks without being intimate sexually.

One day, I came home from work and my daughter told me my husband had unplugged the jack from the wall because he didn't want them on the phone. At this point, my kids hated him. He talked *at* them, not *to* them. In their opinion, he was always complaining about something. Once again, I was furious. Everything that I was holding in came out.

I got on the phone with a friend and complained about how less of a man he was since he wasn't able to provide for his family. My kids didn't like him and we didn't make love any more. While I was upstairs on the phone talking to my friend, he was downstairs on the phone, talking to his sister about everything going on in our household. The next day, he decided to move out and go live with his godbrother.

That's when I knew my marriage was on life support. I tried to save my marriage. I asked him to go to counseling, and he refused. He just wanted space. He just needed time to get his thoughts together. His godbrother stayed in Westland at the same apartment complex where he worked. So, he spent a lot of time hanging out with him, drinking and smoking. We talked on the phone every day; however, he wasn't sold on trying to save the marriage. I talked to my mom on the phone and cried to her about how I messed up. This was all my fault.

"Listen! Don't beat yourself up over this. You're a great wife and mother!" she told me. "Since he has moved out already, and he doesn't want to save the marriage, let him file for divorce."

A year passed and we were still separated, living in two different households. We talked on the phone once a week, if that. I could no longer blame myself. We were both in the marriage. We had a responsibility to each other and to God. After all the crying, praying and blaming,

I enrolled in school and completed my bachelor's degree in business. I got a better job and moved on with my life.

One day, my brother-in-law called me.

"Have you spoken to your husband?" he asked.

"No. I haven't spoken to him in months," I said.

"Well, you need to talk to him because he has something he needs to tell you."

I reached out to him, but he never answered or returned my calls. After a week, I called my brother-in-law to let him know I wasn't able to get in touch with my husband.

"What was it that he is supposed to be telling me?" I asked.

"He has a baby on the way with a young lady who stays in the apartment complex where he's been working."

I was numb!

My heart dropped to my feet.

I instantly became *bitter*.

"He told me this three weeks ago, sis," my brother-in-law continued. "I told him that he needs to tell you about it."

That's why he didn't want to save the marriage. He had created another family while he was working at that apartment complex. Shortly after I found that out, I filed for divorce.

My husband never reached out to me. He never showed up to court for the divorce proceeding.

Years later, my family was over at my brother-in-law's house and an argument broke out. My daughters told my family that my ex-husband molested them when they were younger. It turns out that they didn't tell me because they thought I wouldn't do anything. That night, I cried and felt so stupid. How was I so blinded by love that I'd missed this?

My heart was not healed. Even though years had passed, and I had moved on with my life, my heart was still damaged. Still broken. Still destitute. After all the hurt and pain that this man had caused me, he'd mentally and physically abused my children, as well. I've always loved and treated his oldest daughter like she was my own. But I hated him and the daughter he had with the other woman while we were still married. I had to do some soul searching to find who I was. I went through a healing process of forgiveness. Anyone could see that, even though we were divorced, even though he was no longer in the home, I was hurting from the inside out from what my ex-husband had done to me and my children.

I asked my children to forgive me. I became celibate and started back going to church. I focused on building my self-esteem, as well as building the bond between me and my children. I listened to their hearts, not just their mouths. As I reflect on all that I went through, the bitterness in me made me better. I became a strong woman, a better mom and grandmother.

In 2015, I got remarried to Robert, a man who knows how to communicate, is very supportive, patient, a hard worker, has a great sense of humor, and who loves God. Our first date was beautiful; on our second date, I invited him to Bible study and he has been a member ever since. When my youngest daughter first met him, she asked him what his intentions with me was.

"Not to be her boyfriend, but one day be her husband," he replied.

Even though all my children were over 21 when we met, he has always had an open-door policy for them to talk to him or ask him any questions. He gives them respect and they respect him as well. Since we both had been married before, we always talk about how we can make our marriage successful. We both agreed to keep God in the center, always be willing to forgive one another, make memories together and stay on the same team. Marriage is hard, but with love, trust, communication, commitment and two walking together as one, marriage can be phenomenal! Today, I am an advocate for happy, healthy marriages. The love Robert and I share has inspired me to create "Fun and Marriage." Fun and Marriage host events for traditional married couples to keep their marriage important and stay together by strategically using solutions, games and time management skills. Marriage is not just a job; it's a ministry.

Fun and Marriage believes in "Making A Recognized Relationship Important And Godly Every day!"

Straight Talk, No Chaser
SELF-REFLECTION

1. Think about a time you were blinded by love so much so that you believed it was real. What caused you to be blinded?

2. If you were in a situation similar to this story, would you want a family member or friend to tell you about a baby your spouse has on the side? Why/why not?

3. Many people wait for their spouses to get out of prison, as opposed to moving on with their lives and forming new relationships. How do you feel about those who wait?

About the Author
➡ Ortavia McClain

Too often, women focus on planning their wedding day instead of planning for a successful marriage. Ortavia McClain was one of those women. She never thought she would go through so much heartache and pain in her first marriage. Little did she know, everything she went through prepared her for the strong woman she is today.

As a wife and mother of five children, and grandmother to 11 grandchildren, she firmly believes that a wife should build her husband up, not tear him down. She believes the two should always be on the same team, keeping the lines of communication open always. More importantly, she knows it's vital to keep God in the center of the marriage in order for it to succeed. Her brokenness and bitterness eventually led to her healing process of forgiveness, positioning her to be the founder and CEO of Fun and Marriage. Fun and Marriage hosts events for traditional married couples to come together and enjoy games, food and fun while living, loving and laughing with their spouse—restoring marriages back to God's original plan for marriage.

For more information or booking, email funandmarriage@gmail.com.

Lost & Found
by Kefentse Booth

When I finally found her, the stars were peeking out of the clouds to witness the attraction.

I spoke a love language that caressed her soul.

Our first kiss made time stop; only real lovers understand this blessing.

It's safe to say, if there is gambling in Heaven, everyone up there is betting on one couple—us.

It was May of 2015, and I was days away from my wedding. I proceeded into my office in regular clothes—a far cry from my two-button business suit, pocket square with lapel pin and Oxford shoes. I received nothing but well wishes as I signed non-compete papers. Surrounded by smiles and prayers, my colleagues sowed blessings into me for my soon-to-be nuptials. I'd made the hard decision to no longer work. I had to get my mother on her feet.

Fifty-one days before my wedding day, my mother was diagnosed with cancer.

What should have been the happiest time of my life was overcast with a storm I wasn't prepared to weather. I reassured my fiancée that I had more than enough saved to take care of us while I was off work tending to my mother. I understood that marriage was scary. I knew it would come with its fair share of challenges. But marrying a man who is unemployed isn't the "happily ever after" life any woman dreams about after her wedding day.

We didn't shack prior to marriage. My fiancée stayed with her parents, and she moved in the day after we consummated our union. I was on borrowed time with freedom as I knew it. I slept at my mother's house often to help her in the middle of the night. But once I married, leaving in the middle of the night to help mom would be different, challenging—to say the least.

Leading up to the ceremony, my mother instilled words of wisdom into me. She gave it to me real and raw: bringing two people, from different worlds, together would be different. It would be work. But she encouraged me to give it my all. To never give up. There was a level of selflessness about my mother, which I also saw in my wife.

Prior to the wedding day, we planned several to-do's as we incorporated life together under one roof. The days were evaporating. I needed to redo my house and make room for my new bride. Less than a month out from the big day, I was doing home renovations like I was a star actor on a thirty-minute special on HGTV. Fallon and I had to compromise significantly. This house needed to be *ours*, not just *mine*.

We created a blueprint to work with the space we had. I pulled the carpet up, showcasing the original hardwood floors. I took all my frustration out on the bathroom, which needed a full renovation. It was just me and a sledge hammer, as I demolished the old tile on the floor and walls. I contracted the work that needed to be done on the roof out to a professional.

Fallon and I laugh now as we look back on our humble beginnings. To the naked eye, the bathroom looks great. It has great functionality. In reality, we picked the wrong contractor. I did my homework. Fallon and I both were familiar with his work. Since he was replacing the roof, and I was pressed for time, I slid the bathroom project onto his plate as well. Little did we know, the contractor was a great project manager, but he wasn't the best carpenter. Days after he'd finished, we noticed misaligned gaps in the tile, toilets that weren't properly bolted down, and a jetted tub that was not hooked up to the electrical. We were livid!

Yet, our life together as we would come to know it was slowly merging. We were both in disbelief that our marriage was just short of peeking around the corner. Fallon handled a lot of things I could not. She understood that I was trying to make this the best day of her life. But, at the same time, I also had to ensure that my mother was healthy enough to witness it. She wasn't being selfish, but she also couldn't understand why the bulk of the family's responsibilities laid on my shoulders alone. I could only love more. In my head, I kept rehearsing the fact that the Bible tells you to leave your mother and father, and cleave to your wife. My wife was first. She was supposed to be first.

The week before we married seemed to be the best week of my fiancée's life. Within a matter of days, she passed her Bar Exam to become a lawyer. She also received a full-time position as a prosecutor, and was sworn in as a lawyer in, what seemed to be, hours. The Lord was shining on her and smiling at her hard work taking shape.

But I was free falling.

My world was supposed to be sunshine and blue skies days before my wedding. Instead, I was sitting with my mother inside a hospital room, watching her protein levels go haywire.

Daily, I headed to my mother's house by 8 a.m. I transported her to dialysis since the chemo side effects caused kidney damage. I'd pick her up around noon to escort her to chemo for a treatment twice a week. I made sure she ate lunch and dinner daily, which was hard due to fact that, many days, food tasted like metal to her. I escorted her to many follow-up doctor appointments, which signified to me that doctors were just bleeding the insurance dry. I would take her back home and rush to the other side of town, just to spend time with my future wife. We finalized seating charts, last-minute revisions and anything else that reared its ugly head to disrupt the wedding.

I was running on fumes.

The day Fallon was sworn in as an attorney, I ran around with my mother all morning and afternoon. I had the contractors at the house, working on the roof and finishing up the bathroom. Fallon called to check on me periodically, but I knew I was running behind schedule. She seemed to understand, but eventually her words said it all.

"Just get here."

I drove feverishly from Detroit to Pontiac, Michigan. I could feel the tension in the air as I hurried to make it. But I was already late. She called once more.

"How far are you?"

I could hear the mumbles in the background, saying, "Start without him."

Yet, she wouldn't! To start one of the most joyous milestones in her life without her future husband would be a cardinal sin. So, she made all her family and friends wait on me. She paused time for me to catch back up to her. Those were the little things that deepened my love for her. She'd chosen to put me first during an occasion that didn't belong to me or us. It was *her* day, but she made it *our* moment.

It was May 23, the day of our ceremony. I smiled at the sun as I headed down to my mother's room. I spent as much time as I could with her before she told me, "Don't worry about me! Enjoy this day with your bride."

I still needed to get my tuxedo jacket from the alterations shop. I had to get my hair cut and make it back in time to take pictures with the groomsmen before anyone ever knew I was out of place. It was risky to cut things so closely, but those were the cards I was dealt.

The wedding was to start at 4 p.m. sharp. I wanted everything to be perfect for my bride. I soon noticed the clock displayed 4:10.

"What's the hold up?" I asked. Everyone and everything was in place and the procession started at 4:15. My brothers walked my mother down the aisle, and I walked down next with the facilitator. As the groomsmen and bridesmaids took their places, the song changed.

My life began to sunset on singleness as the sunshine of marriage rose.

She glided down the aisle with so much happiness, style and grace. I smiled and watched as she gripped her father's arm tightly, knowing that her fairytale, everything she'd ever hoped for, was here. Drones flew in the sky as aerial photos were taken simultaneously as the snapshot took place on the ground. I approached my bride and shook the hand of the man who helped birth this beautiful vessel. She trembled in admiration. The tears fell and it was clear that she needed me. I was her protector now, the person who would have to transform any tearful situation into a hopeful one. I mouthed words of love and dedication before the vows.

The trembling stopped.

In that moment, I knew I was the ease of comfort in her life. Under blue skies on a sunny May day, we married, with family and friends cheering us on.

The day and night were amazing. We danced to amazing music once the food was consumed. So many pictures. So much love in one room. We were grateful for all who came to enjoy our special day.

My life shifted. I now bore the title of that which I'd never known: *husband*.

When we moved in together, we knew one another. But we didn't know all the quirks. We understood that there would be a learning curve. She took my side of the bed immediately, as I made little closet space for her. We catered to one another that first week like neither one of us believed the other was ever independent. Since we didn't initially go on our honeymoon, we stayed home to be under one another for the first few days.

One day, Fallon looked at me and said, "Let's go see your mother." I was dreading it, but I needed to see her. We drove to the other side of town and the look of happiness on my mother's face almost made me cry. Her spirits were high, and she talked about everyone (in her own way) who was at the wedding. We laughed all night—just long enough for me to forget the storm that loomed over my family because of her diagnosis.

While many things changed after marriage, my schedule did not. I still took care of my mother and drove her to all of her appointments daily. Though she was able to drive, I didn't want her to become fatigued behind the wheel. So, I continued to chauffeur her. Fallon worked daily and allowed me to be the best support for my mom. But I knew it was wearing thin on her. She was newly married to a man with no job and no plans for next steps. Yet, she didn't badger me. She gave me my space and time.

As September arrived, I took some time for myself when my oldest brother came into town. I felt like I'd neglected my wife, though. She never demanded my time because of the situation my mother was in, but I felt like I owed it to her. After a couple of days of only phone calls, I called my mother.

She said, "I miss you."

Once I hung up the phone, I over-thought myself to sleep on the couch. When I woke up, I knew something wasn't right. I couldn't touch it. I couldn't put my finger on it, but something was out of place. I sat there, puzzled, as my wife stared at me. Suddenly, I had an urge to go see my mother. The whole time, I felt her spirit. It was calling my name.

I was born on September 16, and my mother never missed her son's birthday. Whether near or far, I always received something from her.

On my birthday that year though, my mother was in and out of consciousness. I erased the date off the nurses' white board, just in case she came to and noticed what day it was. I didn't want her blood pressure to go up because she'd missed telling me, "Happy birthday!" Right by my side, my wife tried everything within her power to make me smile and laugh. Though hunger wasn't present, we went to one of my favorite restaurants to have dinner once visiting hours were over. I received so much love from social media that I spent the rest of the night simply asking everyone for their prayers. That's when I realized that I was standing in the rain emotionally.

But, for this storm, unfortunately, an umbrella wasn't enough.

My mother passed away one late September day in the comfort of her home. She was surrounded by loved ones and friends. I was there to the last breath.

That's when my levees broke.

I wanted more time. I wanted more touches and longer conversations. As I dug my nails into the walls from hurt, my wife rubbed my back and held me in her arms. No words would soothe me, and she understood that at this point. She just held me and let me break down. As I look back, I am so thankful for that touch of love in that moment.

There were two funerals for my mother—one in Detroit and one in Alabama. The process of closing a casket twice is equivalent to super human strength. Through it all, I could find comfort in my wife. In Detroit, she gave me time to process. In Alabama, she held me close as I closed the door on a final chapter. Whether she knew what she was doing wasn't the question. She was right there. She was the crutch that held me up. She was the protection from the evils that preyed on my feeble frame. We were new to marriage and I was a shell of my former self.

In October, I lost my way once the casket closed for the final time. My mentor, best friend and mother was not around to get me through it. I tried to shake the feelings, but I wasn't all there. Fallon knew it. I could barely function or help around the house.

I was distant, to say the least. My wife was in a marriage with a man who'd changed overnight—and not for the better. I could only muster up so many excuses before I settled on complacency.

I didn't care about anyone or anything.

Fallon tried her hardest to break the monotony. She told me to write, but I allowed my thoughts to bottleneck. On the holidays, she pulled me along. But all I truly longed for was the solitude of our home. I was alone in her world, never using the voice I owned to say anything other than, "I love you." I never wondered how she felt.

I was hurt. Hurting.

If a mother is the touch from Heaven, then my wife was an angel with the same pedigree. I knew it was hard trying to spark my fire, but Fallon tried daily. She engaged in the talks that pushed us forward because leaving me alone, accepting this half of a man, wasn't an option. I don't know how long it took. I do know that my wife understands the totality of the concept of staying by my side in life's darkest moments.

One day, I realized that I had another best friend in my wife. It was like the sun came out again. But, this time, it shone differently. In my mother's eyes, I could do no wrong. She supported my intentions, as long as they made sense. Now being married, the steps to make my intentions a reality needed to be complemented by a plan of action. My wife was more technical. She utilizes plans to move a mountain. I, on the other hand, will walk up to the mountain and figure out how to move it once the obstacle presents itself. We had two different approaches; yet, we yielded the same result—the mountain moved!

My first step forward was to find myself again. I'd left pieces of me in Alabama and on the eastside of Detroit. As I collected myself, I went over and beyond for the person who stood tall for me during my darkest moment to date. We needed to get away, and all things pointed to a vacation and honeymoon. Jamaica was our destination of choice.

We booked flights to leave a couple days after Christmas, the first Christmas without my mother. The days I longed for her, I went by her house and could smell her scent in the air. I'd sit on the couch and wait, like she was going to pull into the driveway. I was getting better, but still mourning. After so long, my phone would ring. It was Fallon, checking on me.

I was trapped in a fairytale world within the walls of my childhood home.

I never told my brothers that I wasn't strong enough to host Christmas in her house, but who was I to block them from grieving in their own way? They lived in different states and didn't have access like I did. As Christmas rolled around, my distant behavior returned. I dreaded the fact that I had to have a joyful occasion with a key member now missing. I was in the process of telling myself to start new traditions with my wife, but I had to get through my nieces opening their gifts first.

As I packed for the honeymoon, a feeling of peace came over me. The smile came back as I laughed at the snow in Detroit compared to the 80 degrees in Jamaica we were about to experience.

As the plane took off, and I stared out the window at blue skies, Fallon held my hand. She had a way of knowing when my deep thoughts needed to be interrupted to bring me back to reality. Once we landed, I cascaded around the island with new life and my new wife. I was free from so much, alone with an abundance of gratitude for my wife. Whatever she wanted to do, I was all for it. Yes, I had needs also. But my needs took months away from my marriage, and she never complained. I swam with my wife, knowing I didn't know how to. We booked couple's massages to further relax in paradise. Late night dinner at each one of the resort restaurants to just talk set the tone for a peaceful break from the storm. Nightly, we gazed at the stars and, each night, I found the same twinkling star to say, "Thank you!" to the heavens.

That star reminded me of a conversation I had with my mother.

"Take care of her and show her the way," she told me. My mother made me understand that although we were from two different worlds, but the same city, I had to continually show Fallon how deep my love goes.

"Take care of her and always protect her." The words I heard repeatedly as I stared into Fallon's face. I received wisdom from a queen who crowned me as prince from birth. Standing on the pillars of my mother's knowledge and wisdom, I changed my title to king and my wife's to queen.

The first of the year rolled around. As we settled back into our home, I needed to make headway. I had been out of work for ten months. Yes, I had offers. But those offers didn't offer anything fulfilling. I lived alone prior to her, and her contributions to the household would be an accessory instead of a necessity.

I had a new life and, eventually, a new job. Tomorrow looked brighter. Things felt good. Yet, as the days accumulated in the marriage, something still seemed *off*. We were *sleeping* in a home, but not *living* in our home. We were eating daily, but we didn't cook soulful meals that we could partake of together. We spent money but didn't contribute to the advancement of our marriage financially. We had obstacles many elders don't tell you about. The focal point was my mother's passing.

And we neglected to focus on the other things that pressed the marriage forward.

In our eyes, we were married, but living single. A year into the marriage, we didn't have any new furniture other than a dining room table and chairs. We looked to each other for next steps. I was the head of the household, but I wasn't good at planning. She was the helpmate, but we still moved individually. We tried to compromise, which is harder than it sounds. This was the difference in our two worlds, which really meant we were just different in our ways.

How do you merge two lifestyles to move one union forward? Our debates and lengthy talks seemed everlasting, but we needed to get to work as a unit. We came up with different lists of things for each person to be responsible for.

We worked together.

Yet, we didn't work as a unit.

Marriage is a lot of work. The details of the work vary from union to union. Through my days of being married, I lost myself and still laid next to someone who believed that greater was in me. I looked into the eyes of a woman who saw my soul, even though it was hurting from the time we said our vows. As I longed to fill a void, she walked with me. Closely behind me at times I was searching for shelter from life's storms. She never gave up on me. As the calendar turns its pages, we grow stronger. We make new traditions and honor the old ones that were passed down from previous generations.

I learned to love again. I learned to smile when she makes eye contact and passionately say, "Hello, beautiful!" She is my best friend and the carrier of my soul's transgression. She will not want for anything in the world because I didn't have to look for refuge when I needed it. I just crawled into her arms, and she let me rest in her heart until I was ready to come back to the real world. There are plenty of tough days in marriage. Nowadays, we dance in the rain when the storm brews over the horizon. We've been through death, unemployment and losing ourselves in the first year of marriage—only to find our true identity as husband and wife. I am sure more obstacles will come. But, together as one, we can overcome all.

Give me the Lord's grace and my wife. With that, and that alone, I know joy will be forever present.

Straight Talk, No Chaser
SELF-REFLECTION

1. How would the effects of losing someone important in your life change you or your marriage?

2. Would you be able to "step aside" to allow your spouse time to find their way back to normalcy if they lose themselves? What does that look like?

3. Can you bear the load of managing the family until the roles go back to their perceived normal?

About the Author
➥ Kefentse Booth

Like a classic Picasso painting, his literary genius doesn't just leap off the pages—it gets into the heart and soul of the reader. Mirroring the style and prose of literary greats such as Robert Frost, Langston Hughes and Maya Angelou, Kefentse Booth not only paints vivid pictures with his choice of words—he immerses the reader so deep into the situation at hand that they hardly ever have time to come up for fresh air.

In his debut book, *Miles Traveled Down Love's Highway*, Booth takes readers on a journey of life lessons and the reality of relationships. No matter where readers choose to get on this sensual highway, they will experience pain, pleasure and fiery passion—even if they only read one excerpt. Written from a personal perspective of his past mishaps, mistakes and misfits, Booth strives to intertwine the realistic, yet unexpected love life of the average reader—allowing readers worldwide to not only see themselves but *feel* themselves in the moment. In his sophomore project, *Stranded on Love's Highway*, Booth takes readers on a passionate journey—but drops them off to experience the trip in its fullness. Leaving readers broken down in an emotional situation where a spare and a jack won't do, Booth encourages them to unbuckle the seat belt, get out the car and step into the sensual abyss of love—with no end in sight. As many journey down unchartered territory and unpaved roads of creativity, with every turn of the page, one will find themselves having covered a great distance—yet stranded in the exact same place.

Because of his great love for all things literary, Booth founded Street Light Dreams, LLC, where he cultivates and educates writers to pursue their passion and become published authors.

For more information or to book Kefentse, visit www.kefentsebooth.com.

About
So It Is Written, LLC

We are a full-service content writing and editorial company, designed to assist with your every need as it relates to the written word. Writing and editing can be extremely time consuming. The words on your website, in your book or on your professional resume are crucial to your overall success. They can make or break you.

But, we can help!

So It Is Written, LLC believes in the quality of the written word and drafting content in excellence. Whether it's content for the web, brochures, editing manuscripts for bestselling authors or ghostwriting for the author who just doesn't have the time to complete his/her manuscript, we have what it takes to fulfill your literary needs.

Call us at 313-999-6942 today or email info@soitiswritten.net for more details about our personalized writing and editing services. We look forward to working with you to make your project one of excellence!

About
The Red Ink Conference

Known as the Premier Conference for authors, editors, playwrights and more, this writing conference empowers attendees from around the nation to write, edit and market their next bestseller in excellence. Many of the attendees are indie authors who are just starting their publishing journey. We're inviting aspiring bestsellers, as well as those who want to take their writing to the next level by editing for other indie authors, to join us in this year in one of two locations–or both! Our expert presenters have over 20 years of industry experience and run successful businesses that support indie authors nationwide. We're excited to make a dent in the book publishing world and have our attendees learn new, innovative information that will position them to build a solid platform as an author and speaker. For more information, visit theredinkconference.com.

www.ingramcontent.com/pod-product-compliance
Lightning Source LLC
Chambersburg PA
CBHW070737020526
44118CB00035B/1474